The Good News / Bad News

Guide to New York City's Neighborhoods

Nicholas Franklin · Editor

Shelby Custer • Associate Editor

Printed in the United States of America
First Printing 2012

Good News / Bad News Publishing
P.O. Box 289
Booker, TX 79005
www.goodbadpublishing.com

ISBN: 0-9846132-2-6
ISBN-13: 978-0-9846132-2-9

Contents

Essays About Living in New York

By Amanda Green:

By Zachary Wilson:

Introduction

Before I began putting this book together I had spent very little time in New York. This might suggest I am a poor choice to serve as Series Editor for a guide book about New York City's neighborhoods. Perhaps a little background will ease your mind and give you reassurance that you are in good hands.

At several different times in my life I have contemplated moving to New York City. After college when I was armed with a Liberal Arts degree and (shockingly) no job, Manhattan seemed a potential destination. I moved to Telluride instead. Later I visited the city when looking at law schools and decided Columbia or NYU would be a great match for me. Unfortunately neither school agreed. I was able to eventually become a lawyer without the help of New York, but the lure of the city never really went away. Like many people I contemplated what it would be like to live in the biggest most exciting city in America.

Each time I contemplated moving to New York City I found there was never a resource that told me quite what I wanted to know about moving there. For me, like many others, it is all about choosing a neighborhood. In some perfect fantasy world I could speak one-on-one with someone living in every neighborhood in every borough. Since that is not possible I decided to create the next best thing, not just for myself but for others with a similar point of view. This book is the end result.

Each chapter of the Guide to New York's Neighborhoods is written by a writer with substantial contact with the neighborhood they profile. In many cases they live in that neighborhood or nearby. In some cases they recently moved away. In a couple of instances the writer has been visiting the same neighborhood for years and knows it as well as any local. They were not asked to write reviews of the best restaurants or hotels. There are not shortage of those resources from Yelp to Frommers to Lonely Planet. Instead I asked them to write the story of the neighborhood. Who *lives* there not who visits. Is it young twenty somethings with no kids or are small families more common? Is it more expensive than other places in the city? What types of buildings do people live in? What does the neighborhood look like on a weekend? Those are the kind of questions relevant to me and I expect they are relevant to many who consider moving to New York.

True to the Good News / Bad News format, the profiles are not meant to sound like an advertisement from the Chamber of Commerce. Few things in life are perfect and the neighborhoods of New York are certainly not one of them. The writers have attempted to suggest what it is that appeals to them about living there while being honest about the short comings. What you will find is the city is truly one of compromises.

I have attempted to create some consistency to the structure, while at the same time allowing the writer room to write in their own style and voice. The twenty neighborhoods profiled in this first edition are scattered throughout Manhattan, Brooklyn, and one neighborhood in Queens. It is by no means an exhaustive index of every neighborhood in New York. Still, every neighborhood in this book is worthy of a particular type of person considering where in New York they will set up shop.

In 2009 Jason Fried and David Heinemeier released a book called Rework. In the book they described their business school of thought and how they operate their successful company 37 Signals. The chapter that especially stuck with me was titled "Underdo Your Competition." They suggested that rather than try and top every feature your competition is rolling out, instead focus on what you do best and be proud of it. Every year guide books seem to get thicker and thicker to the point it is hard to even use them. There is just too much there. This book is not like that. The focus is on the neighborhoods and that is all. It won't be for everyone, but I hope it is what some people are looking for and find useful.

Finally, I have made a conscious decision to organize the chapters as I see fit. I do not think anyone will necessarily open the book and read it cover to cover. Rather, I expect there will be a neighborhood you have heard something about, maybe from a friend already there saying it is the "hot place to live" or a newspaper article about a burgeoning scene of some sort. You will use the table of contents to find it, read about it, and from there probably go on to the next neighborhood. In this way I hope you will discover New York City's neighborhoods the same way I have: through the eyes of a group of talented writers, never knowing which neighborhood I would be reading about next.

--Nicholas Franklin, Editor.

Astoria

Steve Reeder wasn't destined for the Big Apple; he grew up among orange and avocado trees in Southern California. Since then he's been a tumbleweed that's blown through Budapest, Oregon, Austin, London, and China before getting tangled up in NYC. Disappointed by the tacos in Manhattan he relocated to Queens where he mostly eats and complains about the weather, while moonlighting as an attorney in the City.

The Geographic Boundaries

Astoria's flanks the East River to the west, looking across to Manhattan. The northern part of Astoria turns industrial as you pass 20th Ave, while the eastern extremities stretch out towards 50th St. to be taken over by railroad tracks and the Brooklyn-Queens Expressway (BQE) far from where anyone much cares. Long Island City starts somewhere just south of 36th Ave. Note that you're in Queens now so avenues descend south to north, and streets rise west to east

The Good News

1. *Diversity.*
It is a small world after all, and Astoria brings in residents from all over it. The streets are filled with people speaking different languages, folks wearing exotic clothes, and the savory smells of delicious foreign cuisines. The decision between getting yourself a neighborhood taco or gyro can be a paralyzing one.

2. *Affordability.*
Manhattanites making the jump to Astoria must always ask the same types of questions when calling about housing. Is that price right? For two bedrooms? With a yard? Is there a catch? The answers are usually yes, yes, yes, no. Prices drop precipitously as soon as you get across the river making Astoria's houses and apartments a relative steal.

3. *Down to Earth.*
Don't come to Astoria looking for trendy. People move to Astoria precisely because it's not trendy. This isn't the Gossip Girl New York, so if you want gossip you better make friends with the shawled ladies at the bakery or the mustachioed corner barber. Astoria's laid-back neighborhood feel makes it a great place to grab a beer or a bite without the trouble of getting gussied up.

The Bad News

1. *Lack of Prestige.*

It's unlikely anyone would call a little slice of Astoria a power address. In fact, pack your thick skin on move in day. Most New Yorker's view of Queens is from directly down their noses. If you are looking to brag to that rival back in high school about how you're living it up in NYC it might be best to keep that Queens address a secret.

2. *Distance.*

Sure, the train can take you straight to Midtown, and getting to the East Village is a relative breeze. But if you have friends over in Tribeca it might be better to send a postcard than plan brunch. Good luck getting people to visit you for any reason other than a pretty summer day at the beer garden. For the sake of your social life master the phrase "let's meet somewhere in between."

3. *Aesthetics.*

You know those pretty brownstones where people fall in love on the steps in every New York romantic comedy? Those aren't in Astoria. There are cute tree-lined streets around some corners, and lovingly tending balconies and porches. You will appreciate these touches all the more when you compare them to the too common 1950's storefronts and tacky marble flourishes. Perhaps only in Astoria do paved over plazas with an awkward bust of Socrates count as a park.

Astoria

One can only wonder what Astoria's most famous fictional resident, Archie Bunker, would think of the old neighborhood today. This western slice of Queens has become arguably the most diverse neighborhood in the most diverse borough in one of the most diverse cities in the world. While traditionally home to New York's Greek population, modern Astoria's ethnic Babel now reads like a meeting of the United Nations; Cypriots, Brazilians, Mexicans, Colombians, Bangladeshis, Egyptians, Bosnians, and Japanese all shop at the neighborhood's fruit stands side by side and get along peachy. But perhaps the most dramatic wave of immigration over the past few years has been from across the East River. Young professionals have increasingly begun to settle in this consciously unhip neighborhood and leave their imprint, leaving some to wonder whether Astoria is the new Brooklyn. One thing is for certain, locals sure hope not.

The self-proclaimed heart of Astoria is the pumping commercial artery of 30th Avenue, but both Ditmars Boulevard and Broadway Boulevard have some soul of their own. Dedicated (perhaps deaf) shopkeepers also tend to restaurants and stores up and down 31st Street which runs both directions under the NQ's elevated track. 31st Avenue.

has increasingly become the epicenter of Astoria's gentrification, while on the opposite extreme Steinway Street. is a busy commercial drag that houses fast food outlets and, above 30th Avenue, Astoria's Little Egypt.

Astoria is caught somewhere between two New Yorks. While Astoria might be derided by the rest of Queens as the most "Manhattan" corner of the borough, it will never carry the caché of an address across the river either. Instead, Astoria has forged its own identity as an educated, cultured, yet unpretentious place all its own. While it might not attract celebrities, it has produced a few of its own. Before he left his heart in San Francisco, Tony Bennett grew up in Astoria, as did the ever creepy Christopher Walken. Today legions of lesser known actors and comics call Astoria home, attracted by cheap rents and proximity to Kaufman Astoria Studios which spans numerous blocks on 34th Avenue. Though the studio's more famous address is probably Sesame Street.

Astoria is a relatively cheap place to live for singles and families (and muppets) alike. One would be hard pressed to find a 1-bedroom over $1500. Mutli-room houses can be found for as much as a 1-bedroom in Manhattan. The housing undergoes quite a transformation as one rides the N-train to its northern terminus. While the southern reaches of Astoria are dominated by large brick apartment complexes, the buildings begin to shrink down and streets become tree-lined as one heads north. A jumble of pre-war apartment buildings, row houses, and the occasional new condo are taken over by single family homes near Ditmars Boulevard. There backyards and porches belie the fact that you're still in New York City. But be aware that the architecture isn't always pretty. A few too many Astoria exteriors scream "I was thrown up in the 70's" and are hiding shag carpets like a dirty secret.

30th Avenue has been called one of the grandest restaurant strips in the city. It offers a dizzying array of ethnic eats. Most prominent are the Greek-style cafes with sidewalk seating, frothy frappés, people-watching, and brusque service. Ovelia (3401 30th Avenue) is a welcome exception, and offers great modern Greek food that isn't your YaYa's cooking. Slightly removed is Vesta Trattoria and Wine Bar (2102 30th Avenue). Both offer unconventional Italian like a brunch special "Hangover Pizza" topped with fried egg. Sabroso Mexican grub can be found down the block at El Athens Grill (3011 30th Avenue), a taqueria named after the Greek Capital. Only in Astoria. For Greek seafood that tastes like it came straight from the Aegean, Taverna Kyclades (33-07 Ditmars Boulevard) has huge portions fit for Poseidon himself. On a newly bustling 31st Avenue. you can grab organic bison burgers (Bare Burger, 3321 31st Avenue), a lavish spread of Cypriot tapas (Zenon Taverna, 3410 31st Avenue) and hipster wine and panini in a back garden (Il Bambino, 3408 31st Avenue) all within a block of each other. Steinway Street's Little Egypt has its own stretch of Middle Eastern and North African restaurants. The most notable is

Kebab Cafe (2512 Steinway Street), run by effusive Egyptian philosopher and pharaoh of the kitchen Ali.

Ask any Manhattanite about Astoria's nightlife and you're sure to get one response: beer gardens. Astoria now has two, the "old" and "new." The "old", and still the best, is the Bohemian Hall and Garden (2919 24th Avenue) which just recently celebrated its 100th anniversary. The "new" is the sleek Studio Square (35-33 36th Street) which attracts a little more fratty crowd for outdoor swilling. But Astoria nightlife has grown beyond the garden concept. Sweet Afton (3009 34th Street.) collects all of Astoria's sexiest people into a dim, low-lit bar which would be popular anywhere in Manhattan. The Quays Pub (45-02 30th Avenue) and the Irish Rover (3718 28th Avenue) are both old Queens Irish pubs with brogues and buyback specials. Astoria's ethnic diversity also extends to its drinking options. You'll swear you can speak fluent Spanish after having a few tropical drinks at El Basurero (32-17 Steinway Street.), a Colombian restaurant and bar whose name translates into the "the Garbage Can," which might explain why it's decorated like a Latin TGI Fridays.

While it has every essential that one needs, Astoria isn't conventionally known as a shopping destination. The situation is improving with a handful of boutique shops offering vintage clothes (Loveday 31, 3306 31st Avenue) and jewelry and baubles (Candy Plum 3098 36th Street). With no danger of a Whole Foods opening up any time soon, Astoria is a great place to go food shopping the old European way. The United Brother Fruit stand (3224 30th Avenue) is a glowing temple to produce. If you ever need to shop for three different types of dandelion greens, this is the place. Break out the drachmas and have a feta cheese fête at Titan (2556 31st Street), the spotless Greek supermarket. Beware of Greeks bearing gifts, unless it's some of the delicious baklava from Artopolis (2318 31st Street), the neighborhood's favorite Greek sweets spot. If you prefer to drink your calories the Euro Market (3042 31st Street), a Balkan grocery, differentiates itself by having its entire back wall made up of beers from around the world.

The distance from Manhattan to Astoria is more psychological than physical. There has been some public transportation reshuffling (RIP W train), but it's still fairly easy to get to Midtown in about 20 minutes on any of the yellow trains, the N, Q, or the R. If you have friends in Brooklyn you might as well say goodbye unless you own a car. If someone is truly worried about the occasional closed station it's best to be situated between the NQ line (above ground) and RM line (below ground), as one of the two is almost always running smoothly.

Despite the decent transport, the drawback to living in Astoria is often loneliness. If you can get your friends out to Astoria from the city you're qualified to be a dentist, because it's best described as pulling teeth. Also expect occasional put downs for living in Queens from people who have never even been there. If your self-worth isn't attached to having a Manhattan zip code and you've got a book for the N-train ride home Astoria is a wonderful place to live. No, it's not trendy, but then that's the way Astorians like it.

The Meatpacking District (MPD)

Millie Kerr is a lawyer, freelance writer, and wildlife enthusiast/conservationist. An intense love of sleep lurks behind her professional ambition and seemingly endless energy. Millie has lived in Texas, North Carolina, London, Manhattan, Washington D.C. and Namibia, where she has worked dreadful hours as an office drone, helped to craft regulation for the federal government, blogged endlessly about travel and leisurely pursuits, fed and slept alongside cheetahs and lions, and, whenever possible, cultivated awkwardness and many amusing anecdotes (all of which are true, even the ones about lions and cheetahs).

The Geographical Boundaries

The traditional Meatpacking boundaries are as follows: 14th Street on the North; Hudson Street on the East; Gansevoort Street on the South; and the Hudson River on the West. Recent expansion creates blurry lines, and some would extend the area as far North as 16th Street.

The Good News

1. Great location.
Meatpacking's proximity to the Hudson River, West Side
Highway and newly erected High Line are all enviable. Some
of lower Manhattan's best streets and offerings sit nearby in
the neighboring West Village.

2. Outstanding amenities.
Two ultra-swanky hotels book-end great restaurants, art
exhibitions and shops, and they all comprise a small,
pedestrian-friendly area.

3. Interesting vibe.
Meatpacking exudes an "up and coming vibe" that attracts
creative folks and ventures. Examples includes high-end
fashion retailers (DVF, Alexander McQueen), transformative
art (Whitney Gallery downtown expansion alongside
polished graffiti) and architecture (The Standard Hotel, the
High Line), and powerful commercial residents (both Google
and Apple have their NYC bases in the Meatpacking
District).

The Bad News

1. Few residential options.

Once abandoned warehouses now house stylish stores, museums, restaurants and night clubs, leaving limited space for modest shoeboxes that better accommodate budget-conscious New Yorkers.

2. Trendy & Touristy.

The aforementioned "interesting vibe" brings with it certain unpleasant features, some of which nauseate down to Earth personalities. European men wearing tight and cropped jeans abound as do hipsters sporting sunglasses…indoors. Night clubs are guarded by arrogant bouncers, who give priority to celebrities, hair gel and short skirts. During weekend nights, MPD becomes an unpleasant caricature (Jersey Shore meets Eurotrash meets Lindsay Lohan).

3. Unnecessarily expensive.

MPD residents often prefer to venture to the West Village for drinking and eating, where myriad eateries provide delicious, affordable fare in a city where nothing comes cheap. MPD's expansion has boxed out small, homegrown business owners, leaving a few memorable places alongside overhyped, overpriced spots.

The Meatpacking District

I first became acquainted with modern day Manhattan through television and film. Seinfeld, Woody Allen, and Candace Bushnell walked me through New York—its gritty streets, cozy restaurants and stranger-than-fiction characters —before I was old enough to experience the city on my own. My exceptions to this media-centric relationship were occasional family trips from Texas, the majority of which were devoted to museums and theater, staples of midtown Manhattan.

The Meatpacking District was certainly never on my radar during those vacations, when we'd see jocose musicals and dine at the 21 Club, Cole Porter songs still dancing through our minds. Just as my parents had crafted their own version of Manhattan, one that no doubt paid homage to their parents' generation, I had to create mine many years later. Unsurprisingly, my first acquaintance with the now extremely hip borough was through pop culture, when Sex and the City's Samantha Jones moved into a Meatpacking loft. You've all seen the episode: Samantha adores her light-filled, spacious bachelorette pad, until she discovers that transvestite prostitutes gather beneath her window nightly, when they make a cacophonous ruckus.

Compared to the West Village, a neighborhood with a genuinely residential vibe, Meatpacking remains faithful to its commercial roots despite many dramatic shifts. A century ago, Meatpacking housed some 250 packing plants and slaughterhouses, the gradual departure of which left many large warehouses vacant yet intact. Criminals, scoundrels and party people seized on the abandoned area where they could behave near-anonymously. Business and pleasure were conducted in clubs and darkened alleyways.

Its grimy past has all but vanished, but MPD is still funky, even though its street graffiti and businesses are now owned by big corporations. Like Google and Apple, two of the powerful additions to the neighborhood, MPD is navigating a precarious balance between its underground past and a stable, albeit corporate, future. Although MPD lacks the charm and camaraderie of other New York neighborhoods, it is best viewed as a complement to the West Village and Chelsea. These are places where residents can better find balance and connection within their community.

My inner epicurean is satisfied by a multitude of restaurants in lower Manhattan—a gastronomical Mecca—although the MPD venue depends in large part on the occasion. For casual brunches or weeknight dinners, I prefer the Standard Bar & Grill, Paradou (aim for the outdoor garden area), Son Cubano (live music and salsa dancing), and Bill's Bar and Burger. Some of my other favorite casual eateries reside on the fringes of Meatpacking: Café Gitane (quaint Parisian café in the Jane Hotel); La Taza de Oro (Puerto Rican cuisine); the Fatty Crab (Malaysian); and the Spotted Pig (extremely popular European gastro pub).

Low-key drinks are shared at the Standard Beer Garden, Gaslight, or over foosball and board games at 675 Bar. Brass Monkey is my go-to dive, with a younger crowd that takes me back to my college days. Formal evenings, occasion-driven or not, are spent at the Homestead steakhouse, or over Italian cuisine at Valbella or the newly opened Scarpetta. Nights of every variety can be concluded at the nearby Diner, where greasy disco fries work wonders to prevent hangovers (open 'til 6am on Saturdays).

Shopping in the Meatpacking District is civilized compared to more dense touristy areas like Soho and 5th Avenue. Stores are spacious and walking between them is easy, but the majority of MPD stores—Diane Von Furstenburg, Alexander McQueen, Stella McCartney, Christian Louboutin are out of any normal person's price range. Some of the more affordable boutiques—like Jeffrey, Scoop and Calypso—lure me in for the occasional accessory splurge, but I prefer to spend my free days meandering along the newly opened High Line.

The High Line—originally utilized as a lifted rail track—was nearly demolished during the 1990s. Dedicated community efforts precluded this fate by offering a unique alternative for the rare space. The result, a sort of raised public park, is loyal to its original purpose and synchronized to contemporary design. Wild, weed-ridden foliage borders the pathway, and wooden seats, some of which link into the original rail tracks, provide visitors the chance to sit and soak up Hudson vistas.

I'm also hugely fond of sharing beers and games of ping-pong at the Standard Hotel Beer Garden. This large semi-outdoor space brings urban zest to the traditional German Biergarten. A variety of foreign and domestic accents buzz across the narrow wooden tables, where people snack on pretzels and pound heavy steins of beer. Adjacent to the beer garden is the Standard Grill, a fantastic, reasonably affordable restaurant that defies the MPD vibe with warmth, traditional décor and food. The burger and fries are absolutely decadent, and lunching there is a welcome alternative to the established spots (Pastis and Barbuto) and the ultra-rowdy Bagatelle (where lunch precedes heavy boozing and dancing typically reserved for nightclubs).

The willingness to pair modernity (epitomized by the hotel structure, lobby and upper level bars) with classic, even retro, features (the Standard Grill and most of the hotel suites) characterizes the Standard's spirit. Creativity is of utmost importance, whether in guest rooms (masculine throw-backs that conjure up images of Hugh Hefner circa 1970) or the upper terraces, one of which includes large mattress-like seats where guests can sip cocktails and watch the sun set, or more likely, rise.

Other late night revelers do the same atop the Hotel Gansevoort, the first contemporary hotel to grace the MPD skyline. Although the Standard and Gansevoort are comparable in size, price, and scene, at least when the metrics are modern and trendy, the two employ distinctive styles. Unlike the retro newcomer, the Gansevoort is 110% modern, its color-scheme dominated by gray and neutral colors (with, of course, the requisite splash of lavender). The Gansevoort rooms are more classic, feminine and spacious than those at the Standard, and the hotel service seems more on cue. What's missing is the Standard's friendliness and edge, or maybe the Gansevoort just feels old in comparison, in a place where newness reigns.

It's fitting that I end my musings, here, with the two landmark MPD hotels. These two structures dramatically changed the MPD landscape, one that is now eternally influenced by their presence, for better or worse. They demonstrate too that the neighborhood caters to vacationers more than locals, this being a neighborhood of fantasy over fiction...either a liberating or depressing realization depending on your intentions.

Fort Greene

Jason Ed Collins is finishing his novel, a noir set in Prague, while getting his MFA in Fiction at The New School. You can see his musical and motorbike projects at the following website: www.combustedass.com

Fort Greene

Fort Greene pulses with a rhythm like no other neighborhood in Brooklyn, New York. If you listen closely, you hear more than the driving beats moving heads and feet in one of its trendy bars; you hear more than the thumping hip hop streaming out of passing cars; you hear the battle cries and beating war drums of American History. Situated in northern Brooklyn, Fort Greene was once host to a fort during the American Revolution. Built in 1776, Generals Nathanael Greene and George Washington shared command over the fort during the Battle of Long Island. The Americans lost the battle. Washington retreated at night to avoid annihilation and saved as many soldiers as he could. After winning the war, the fort fell into decay. Walt Whitman was instrumental in creating a park on its former grounds. Frederick Law Olmstead and Calvert Vaux later redesigned the park, the first in Brooklyn. The Prison Ship Martyr's Monument and vault were later erected to house some of the bones of the 12,000 American Prisoners of War, who washed ashore from the British war ships docked in neighboring Wallabout Bay. The monument, once the tallest Doric column in the world, has lately been restored, bejeweling the apex of the lush, hilly park.

By 1850, Brooklyn's population had swollen from 4,000 to 100,000 inhabitants, many of whom took root in Fort

Greene. Local farmers distributed land parcels for construction, giving rise to the building boom of Italianate brick and brownstone row houses, most of which remain preserved to this day. The neighborhood has since been known for its airy, tree-lined streets and its beautiful low-rise housing. The Williamsburg Savings Bank Tower, one of the ten greatest skyscrapers in New York, was built from 1927 to 1929, just before the Great Depression halted further high rise construction.

Fort Greene is bordered by Flatbush Avenue to the west, Vanderbilt Avenue to the east, Myrtle Avenue to the north and Atlantic Avenue to the South. Its major arteries are Myrtle Avenue and Fulton Street.

While strolling along one of its redolent sidewalks, one might bump into one of the many celebrities who hang their hats in Fort Greene. Once home to Walt Whitman, John Steinbeck, Truman Capote and Richard Wright, Fort Greene now hosts the likes of Kerri Russell, Talib Kweli, Erykah Badu, Jhumpa Lahiri and Colson Whitehead.
Spike Lee operated his production company, 40 Acres & A Mule, in Fort Greene. Many entertainers, politicians, artists and writers of the Black community are proud to live in the neighborhood.

Attractions

The Brooklyn Academy of Music was rebuilt in Fort Greene in 1908 after the original in Brooklyn Heights burned to the ground.   It hosts world-class theatre, cinema, music and dance. Reigning as New York City's home for progressive and avant garde performance, artists as diverse as Philip Glass, Peter Brook, Laurie Anderson, Lee Breuer, ETHEL, Nusrat Fateh Ali Khan, Steve Reich, Seal,Nirvana, Alice in Chains, Robert Wilson, BLACKstreet, Ingmar Bergman, The Whirling Dervishes, and Cate Blanchett have graced its stages.

Myrtle Ave, to the north, and Fulton Street, to the south, remain the epicenters of restaurants and night life. Many of Brooklyn's most notable establishments call Fort Greene home: Chez Oskar, Madiba, the Habana Outpost, the Smoke Joint, the Cake Man, the relatively new German beer garden, Der Schwarze Koelner. Any cuisine desired can be found along one of its sidewalks. Specialty coffee shops abound. And at night the energy cranks at places like Moe's, a premier bar and lounge, Alibi, the General Greene and Rope. Whatever the flavor, swanky, divey, hood or hip, Fort Greene delivers.

Weekend afternoons are comfortably filled with perusing the wares at the local book and clothing boutiques, strolling the aisles of one of the neighborhood's notable flea markets, playing a game of soccer or tennis in Fort Greene Park, or sidewalk dining at one of the many brunch hotspots. Meanwhile, the pleasures of Williamsburg remain a short train or cab ride away, and attractions in Park Slope and Prospect Heights are well within walking distance.

Housing

Housing stock in Fort Greene generally consists of brick or brownstone row houses. The occasional carriage house spots the cityscape. And with the renovation of The Williamsburg Savings Bank Tower, high-end condominiums are readily available. While renting and buying prices remain cheaper than Manhattan, they are rather high for Brooklyn. Prices are comparable to the neighboring Park Slope.

Demographics

Fort Greene's been publicly noted for its diversity. The sidewalks are crowded with professionals, creatives, manual laborers, students, artists, the elderly, stay at home moms pushing strollers, and the working and non-working poor. People of color live alongside Caucasians in a relative harmony that confounds many. And, while the neighborhood has faced some of the pressures of gentrification, it seems as though it will forever retain the local flavor of the Black community responsible for restoring its prominence in the 1990s.

Transportation

Resting at the nexus of the borough, it's hard to match the transportation in Fort Greene. Most every subway line in New York City runs through the neighborhood: the B, D, N, Q and R at DeKalb Avenue; the 2, 3, 4, 5, B, D, N, Q and R at Atlantic Pacific Street; the A and C at Lafayette Avenue; the G at Fulton Street; and the LIRR at Flatbush Avenue.

The Downsides

The near-Manhattan pricing for groceries, daily goods and attractions has become a downside in Fort Greene. Additionally, while the crime associated with the public housing north of Myrtle Avenue has been mitigated in the past two decades, it still remains a slight issue to this day.

In Closing

Fort Greene couples its attractions with elegant housing and airy, tree-lined streets. It not only boasts a colorful past, but it's sure to boast continuing splendor in the future. All things considered, many commuters, as well as those who live and work in the neighborhood, find themselves hard-pressed to name a better place to live.

Clinton Hill

Jason Ed Collins is finishing his novel, a noir set in Prague, while getting his MFA in Fiction at The New School. You can see his musical and motorbike projects at the following website: www.combustedass.com

Clinton Hill

Clinton Hill, a neighborhood in Northern Brooklyn, New York, wears many faces. Saddled by Fort Greene to the west, Bed-Stuy to the east, Wallabout Bay to the north and Prospect Heights to south, Clinton Hill remains a mélange of the old and new, fusing the variegated influences pressing upon it from all sides. The diversity of architecture reflects the neighborhood's diverse population. Clinton Hill boasts having one of the highest concentrations of Post-Civil-War row houses in the country. Walking down Clinton Avenue, you might bump into Rosie Perez or Mos Def. You might even channel the poetry of Walt Whitman, a neighborhood resident while he was writing Leaves of Grass. Visitors and residents, alike, take time to admire the four mansions 19th Century millionaire Charles Pratt built for himself and his sons. Farther down Clinton Avenue's slate sidewalks, a host of other stately structures (built by New York City's wealthy in one of their first waves of migration from Manhattan to Kings County) rise along each side of the street until Myrtle Avenue. At the conclusion of the stretch, cocktails and a bite to eat can be had at the conveniently located Maggie Brown's.

Attractions

Myrtle Avenue and Fulton Street, to the south, remain the loci of activity. Restaurants serving cuisines from all over the world pepper each of the major thoroughfare's sidewalks. Spliced amongst the international dining establishments, clothing boutiques and beauty stores rise along with tire shops and hardware depots, with little apparent logic beyond an elapsed lease having lent entry to another immigrant group. Up and down Fulton Street and Myrtle Avenue, one sees the seedlings of gentrification struggling to sprout amidst a resistant contingent that refuses to be pushed out. Within a few steps on Fulton Street, one can choose between first rate Ethiopian food and Popeye's Southern Fried Chicken. Hipsters get their grunge and indie fix from the jukebox at Rope, sipping Pabst Blue Ribbons and shots of Beam. A few doors down on Myrtle Ave, a couple professionals share a bottle of Valpolicella and Italian eats in Anima's redolent courtyard. Meanwhile, across the street, heads are bouncing to the freshest hip hop track with Heinekens in hand.

Minutes away, the Brooklyn Academy of Music and Fort Greene's blocks and blocks of restaurants, bars and boutiques offer a lifetime of entertainment. Lazy afternoons can be passed strolling Bed-Stuy's lanes of bookstores, boutiques and coffee shops. The music, food and art of Williamsburg remain a short train ride away. The restaurants flowering all over Prospect Heights open their doors just minutes south of Clinton Hill's shady streets.

After returning to the neighborhood, one can stroll through the grounds of the Pratt Institute, marveling at its sprawling sculpture garden. And on days of worship, one can attend services at any number of beautiful churches that serve a myriad of denominations.

Housing

Clinton Hill offers housing options for those of any income level. It's a singular neighborhood for its shared presence of Pre-Housing-Collapse Condos (units still available), centuries-old row houses, townhouses and beautiful brownstones, occasional wood shingled abodes and high-occupancy housing projects. Strangely, Clinton Hill is home to almost every type of residential structure found in Brooklyn. Aside from the bustle on Fulton Avenue and Myrtle Avenue and the commotion on Pratt's campus, most of the neighborhood remains residential. Once off the major Avenues, quiet nights of restful sleep await. Whether renting or buying, prices are cheaper than the neighboring Fort Greene. In fact, Clinton Hill offers some of the more agreeable rental and purchase prices in the cluster of centrally located, Brooklyn neighborhoods.

For those in the market, beware of paying Fort Greene prices for a room or apartment properly located in Clinton Hill. Attempts to capitalize on Fort Greene's name, former and present occupants and sidewalk flare, have nowadays stretched once firm boundaries farther east into Clinton Hill. Despite those notions, Clinton Hill remains bound by

Vanderbilt Avenue on the west, Classon Avenue on the east, Park Avenue on the north and Atlantic Avenue on the south.

Demographics

Clinton Hill is a bubbling cauldron of mixed classes and ethnicities. The sidewalks are crowded with professionals, creatives, manual laborers, students, artists, the elderly, stay at home moms pushing strollers, and the working and non-working poor. People of color live alongside Caucasians, as well as Latinos and the occasional Hassidic Jew further east. Students flock to housing around St. Joseph's College and the Pratt Institute.

Transportation

The C train and the G train service Clinton Hill. Additionally, a host of bus routes roll through the neighborhood: the B25, B26, B38, B45, B48, B52, B54, B57, B61 and B69.

The Downsides

While Clinton Hill remains an affordable, welcoming neighborhood, there are a few downsides that any visitor or potential resident should consider. The first downside is transportation. Clinton Hill remains centrally located in Brooklyn. However, the C train and the G train, which rolls only in Brooklyn, prove to be a few of the least desirable train lines in the city. Residents working above downtown Manhattan are known to change trains as many as two times to get to their places of employment.Fortunately, a short walk or bus ride to Fort Greene offers access to most any train line in the city.

The second downside is crime—not that it's prevalent. However, the demographic mixture has at times led to tension, particularly between long term residents and the relatively affluent Pratt student body.

In Closing

Clinton Hill might not have the mass appeal of other destination neighborhoods. But for those looking for an airy, tree-lined place to hang their hat, it fits the bill. Its beauty and quiet streets offer a welcomed retreat from New York City life.

Williamsburg

Jennifer McPherson is native Southern Californian writer living on the mean streets of New York City. A former Williamsburger, she now lives in the West Village and likes to brag about it to anyone who will listen. Jen is a contributing writer for a slew of humor, travel and health sites (ask her anything about cancer, seriously) and an improv performer / cast member in New York's Accomplice: The Show.

The Good News

1. Music Scene.

Williamsburg became the Williamsburg that it is today because of the influx of starving artists and the music scene. Brooklyn's trendiest borough hasn't waned. The Music Hall of Williamsburg continually showcases the kind of bands that are just hitting the brink of fame. Smaller venues maintain the coffee shop atmosphere that up and coming artists have always come to New York for.

2. Food.

There are too many extraordinary restaurants in Williamsburg to count, but there are an awful lot of places that consistently win awards for just one neighborhood. Some restaurants have have people flocking the L Train into Brooklyn on a daily basis. And because the demographic of Williamsburg is overwhelmingly under-30, the restaurants are consistently packed and full of bustle.

3. The Space.

While the rent is starting the rival Manhattan, you definitely get much more bang for your buck in Williamsburg. The same amount of money will get about 1.5 times more space or more depending how far east or south you live. And, the streets have actual trees, relatively low street traffic and residents report a significantly lower chance of being hit by a cab, bus or biker on their way to get coffee.

The Bad News

1. Hipsters.

They're everywhere in this part of town. They leave a snail trail of cheap beer, facial hair and judgment all over the streets. And, there's no time of day you can escape them because most of them are artists (i.e. they don't have a job). You will never be able to score a pair of skinny jeans in a thrift shop in Williamsburg. You will never see anything like "sunbathing" in McCarren Park for the rest of your life. And, you will feel old pretty much everywhere you go. Even the 50 years olds in this neighborhood wear converse and t-shirts with a giant thumbs up on them.

2. The L Train.

It really is the best of times and the worst of times on the L. But, when it's bad, it's the worst train in the city. It shuts down at night and on weekends like clockwork every winter. When the train is working, it is always jam packed.

3. Aesthetic.

Williamsburg is one of the ugliest neighborhoods in New York City. There are abandoned warehouses and factories every where. The new condos are hideous and the old brick apartment buildings are run down. Every time you walk home from a bar and make a wrong turn, you end up walking into what looks like the beginning of a horror film. The streets on Saturday and Sunday around Bedford Ave are covered in a sea of cigarettes, urine and bad decisions.

Williamsburg

Williamsburg is a neighborhood in the north section of the Brooklyn borough of New York City. It is bordered by Greenpoint, Bushwick, Bedford-Stuyvesant and the East River. Since its annexation into the city of New York proper, Williamsburg has morphed from an ethnically diverse melting pot, to an industrial wasteland of drugs and crime, to what it is today: the hipster capital of the world.

History

The Dutch acquisition of Williamsburg was annexed into the Eastern District of Brooklyn in 1855. Many of New York's wealthiest people built mansions along the banks of the East River in Williamsburg as a refuge from the city. Taking a cue from the likes of Vanderbilt, Fisk and Pratt, a slew of industrial tycoons looked to the Williamsburg waterfront to build enormous factories in the southern section of the neighborhood. At one point in the 19th century, Williamsburg held ten percent of the entire nation's wealth.

The opening of the Williamsburg Bridge in 1903 marked an influx of immigrants, who were looking to flee the heinous living conditions of the tenements and ghettos of lower Manhattan. The combination of better living conditions and easily accessible factory work cemented Williamsburg's position as the hub of New York's international working class. Soon enough, however, Williamsburg became the most densely populated neighborhood in New York, and living conditions proved to be no better than the lower east side. By post-World War II, the neighborhood became synonymous with drugs and crime, and it stayed that way for decades.

The Artists

In the 1970s, many artists began to move into the neighborhood for the dirt-cheap rent. The abandoned factories were illegally rented as live-work loft spaces. The influx continued and, by the mid-1990s, Williamsburg was becoming known for drugs and ground-breaking music, performance art and painting. It was still dirty and dangerous, but it had a "cool" factor that no other neighborhood had at the time. As a result, more and more young artists flocked to the area to join the scene.

The Jewish

During World War II, a massive influx of Hasidic Jews moved to Brooklyn to escape Hitler (naturally). Currently, there is an enormous population of the Satmar Hasidic sect living in South Williamsburg (south of Broadway). They stick to their own, for the most part, and they would be almost unnoticeable if they didn't often get into altercations with people for refusing to move out of the way of bike traffic.

The Hipsterfication

Today, Billburg (as the kids are calling it) is the most notable hipster community in the world. While there are still many artists who reside in the neighborhood, the increase in popularity amongst young people has caused rent to rise to the point it now rivals Manhattan. The true artists have been pushed further east into Brooklyn. What has come to take the artists' place is nothing short of horrendous. The area around Bedford Avenue (the main Billburg thoroughfare) is entirely inundated with trust-fund kids who don't shower, don't work and don't get past noon sober. They have little to do with creation but wholeheartedly refer to themselves as part of the artist community. To their credit, however, hipster fashion choices have been mimicked from Silver Lake in Los Angeles to China and their presence is responsible for maintaining what is, arguably, the best restaurant, bar and music scene in the city.

The Scene

Williamsburg is notorious for its music culture. Zebulon, Pete's Candy Store and The Music Hall of Williamsburg have been responsible for maintaining the presence of up and coming bands. Many musicians, who have already found popularity or fame, repeatedly visit the venues for intimate concerts as a "thank you" to the community for helping them get their start. On any given night of the week, the music venues and bars off of the Bedford stop are packed with people watching the next big thing no one has heard of...yet. It's incredible because of the energy and enthusiasm the community has towards the music scene. It can be awful, however, because it can turn into a frat party quickly. Pabst Blue Ribbon cans and cigarette butts line the streets, where weeds don't dare to grow.

Union Pool is a neighborhood staple that, in the words of its actual owner, "if a tidal wave hit this place on a Monday night, the skinny jean population of New York would be down by 70 percent." It has a great back patio, and it boasts some of the best people watching in town. But, it truly is a meat market for the morose, judgy and unemployed.

Hotel Delmano, another one of Billburg's staples, is Union Pool's mortal antithesis. It is beautiful, dark and old timey. They have great jazz bands on weekend evenings and a cocktail menu that rivals any Manhattan mixology venue.

Spuyten Deyvil has a beer list so long it's overwhelming, and the bartenders aren't what anyone would refer to as helpful or even polite. On the other hand, the patio, along with selection, makes it the best place for a relatively tranquil evening that the neighborhood has to offer.

The Food

Williamsburg has had an explosion of hip and trendy restaurants in the last ten years. Motorino has been voted the best pizza in New York by nearly every big magazine. Diner and Marlow and Sons both have incredible menus of food that is all organic and from sustainable local farms. Moto shines not only in ambience and food but also because it's off the beaten path (it's located far away from people who will judge someone for having no visible tattoos).

Living

The apartments in the Bedford Avenue area are a combination of run-down railroad walk-ups that fifteen Pratt students live in and new luxury condos that are predominantly vacant (aside from squatters). The best living conditions are further east, along Lorimer and Graham Avenues. There is more of an adult neighborhood feel around these streets and it's significantly cleaner. The rent is now too high in all of Williamsburg proper for most of the actual artists, but there are enough to maintain the neighborhood's edgy reputation.

The plus-side (living arrangement-wise) of living in Williamsburg is that, although the rent nearly equals that of Manhattan, the size of the apartments is, generally, much larger. The buildings, for the most part, tend to be older, but there are a lot of new elevator buildings sprinkled throughout the neighborhood. Furthermore, the streets (outside of Bedford) are much quieter than Manhattan, so no one has to worry about being kept up all night by ambulances, foot traffic, cabs honking, etc.

Transportation

The L train is the subway line that runs through the main part of Williamsburg, and it is the best of times and the worst of times. When it's "on," the L is the fastest and most reliable train in the city. When it's not -- several times a year -- it can be delayed for an hour or just not running at all. This can pose a major problem for people trying to get into Manhattan in the dead of winter. The JMZ line connects south Williamsburg to the Lower East side. It isn't as fast as the L and it's a bit of a hike, but it's above ground for most of the commute, providing somewhat of a pretty ride. The dreaded G train connects Williamsburg to Queens and South Brooklyn. Taking this train requires a copy of Crime and Punishment or any other novel that cannot be finished in less than two hours.

UPPER WEST SIDE

Susan Waggoner moved to New York accidentally with some college friends and fell in love with the city. Convinced she was born to be a New Yorker, she prizes the city for it's constant motion, it's rich and ever-present history, and the vast freedom it offers resident to dream big and compete on the world's most spectacular playing field.

The Good News

1. Brownstones.

The 130 year-old brownstones that line most of the cross streets give the neighborhood an Old New York flavor that's hard not to love. They make the big city small and friendly and if you have a chance to live in one, grab it. The period details are full of charm, the thick walls block out an amazing amount of city noise, you'll end up knowing all your neighbors.

2. Cook's Delight.

The half-mile stretch of Broadway from 71st to 81st Streets is a goldmine for home chefs. Start with Trader Joe's at the south end and proceed north to the ever-expanding Fairway, the Citarella fish and grourmet market, fragrant H&H Bagels, and Zabar's massive delicatessen. And if you have nothing to cook your purchases in, you'll find everything from mushroom brushes to copper chafing dishes on Zabar's mezzanine level.

3. Personality

It's a refreshing surprise to discover that one of the city's coolest zip codes also delivers one of its most relaxed atmospheres. Long the preference of actors, dancers, and writers, the UWS has preserved its free spirit through tsunamis of gentrification and population growth, possibly because Central Park to the east and Riverside Park to the west have kept residents from getting too serious about spike heels and button down collars.

The Bad News

1. High housing prices
Everything desirable about the neighborhood is reflected in the price of housing. Don't bother looking for a bargain fixer-upper here – almost everything that can be renovated has been, and what hasn't is priced as if it were.

2. Unexciting restaurants
Gentrification has removed most of the funkily charming little eateries and replaced them with nothing special. Restaurants come and go frequently, often with great hype, but almost all are ultimately disappointing, combining high prices with mediocre fare.

3. Over-priced Retail Space.
Urban renewal began with Lincoln Center in the 1960s, and the UWS has been getting pricier ever since. This has driven out any number of small but useful stores and replaced them with high-end boutiques, Starbucks, and real estate agents. Plan to drive to Ohio for common items like ironing board covers, kitchen glasses, and throw rugs.

Upper West Side

It Began with Buffalo

The first pioneer of the Upper West Side was the Eastern Wood Bison. In fact, they can be considered to be the first city planners. Their regular migration made a track from the southern end of Manhattan to the north for hundreds of miles. Over time, the track became a path, and the path widened into a trail. Dutch farmers followed it north from New Amsterdam and became the first Europeans to settle, making the old trail a main thoroughfare. George Washington knew the route so well that he could sleep in the saddle all the way to Albany. Known simply as "the Road" at first, it eventually acquired a proper name: Broadway.

As one follows Broadway north from Times Square, the clamor of the city eventually fades. North of 59th Street the land opens up to a sky big enough to demand notice. Skyscrapers are rare, and side streets are residential. Manhattan's Upper West Side runs north from 59th Street to 110th Street and is bordered by Central Park on the east and the Hudson River on the west. To the 228,000 people, who populate Upper West Side, Broadway isn't the "Great White Way" (a nickname for Broadway) at all. It is "Main Street."

From its start, the neighborhood has been revered for its diverse culture, which includes Jews from the Lower East Side, writers and artists attempting to live inexpensively, immigrants from Latin America, and a rebellious performing arts crowd. Those who have called the Upper West Side home include: writers Edgar Allen Poe, Dorothy Parker, James Baldwin, Albert Camus, Sinclair Lewis and Isaac Bashevis Singer; musicians Duke Ellington, Irving Berlin, Bix Beiderbecke and Jerome Kern; and larger-than-life personalities Mae West and Babe Ruth. "The Charleston" (a tune that popularized the Charleston dance) was introduced at a theater on West 63rd Street, as was Noble Sissle and Eubie Blake's "I'm Just Wild About Harry" (an exuberant song that poet Langston Hughes credited for sparking the Harlem Renaissance).

Residents of today's Upper West Side are more likely to be single than married, have completed four or more years of college, work white-collar jobs and earn an above-average income. Young families have recently made a few toeholds; however, many eventually move on, keeping the average age generally under 40 and the average household size small.

How'd Ratso Rizzo Get that Huge Apartment?

In recent years, the Upper West Side has undergone extensive renovation. In the movie "West Side Story" a glimpse of the old neighborhood is provided. Tony and Marie (two main characters) sing where the Lincoln Center now stands. The good news: it's now one of the city's most desirable areas.   The bad news: reasonable rent will never return.

For buyers and renters, apartment hunting is fairly straightforward.   Family-sized apartments can be found in larger buildings on north/south streets and the occasional side street. Central Park West is too expensive for most, but Riverside Drive costs less and has some of neighborhood's most beautiful architecture. West End Avenue is prime hunting ground, as are large buildings along the commercial avenues of Broadway, Amsterdam and Columbus. Remember: buildings with ground floor shops benefit from rental income, which can substantially lower maintenance fees.

Buyers and renters, who don't need a big family space, can often find an apartment in one of the brownstones that line the cross streets. Most have been divided into studios or one

and two bedroom units. While brownstones are full of
character and exposed brick, their lack of elevators,
doormen and space can be a drawback.

For renters, finding an apartment can be particularly
frustrating. The city's rent control, rent stabilization and
free market laws cause rent to reflect the apartment's
turnover rate and renovation history, rather than its
condition or square footage. The city's attempts to restore
sanity have been slow at best. Therefore, an apartment with
fairly stabilized rent is worth paying a premium. For those
who can't find an apartment, subletting is an option. Many
lease-holders live away permanently, and a sizable number
of subletting tenants eventually acquire the lease. Although
the cost of housing is high, close proximity to shops, services
and good public transportation makes owning a car
unnecessary, which inevitably increases savings.

Living La Vida Local

Despite gentrification, the independent, slightly eccentric
spirit of the Upper West Side remains intact. The streets are
lively during the day, with restaurants, stores and several
museums in full swing. At night, there is Lincoln Center's
smorgasbord of classical music, ballet and opera, as well as
the Beacon Theater, a live concert venue. Alongside special
events, most residents simply enjoy their favorite
restaurants, bars, people-watching and walking around the
neighborhood.

Although rare in a city built on rock and made of concrete, the majority of residents have both a front and back lawn and access to parks. Everyone knows Central Park, but equally spectacular is Riverside Park. It's a four-mile swathe of green running north from 72nd Street, along the Hudson River. Walkways, gardens and the city's best biking paths make Riverside Park a hidden gem.

The area has a limited array of traditional grocery stores, but, due to its gourmet markets and specialty stores, it's a cook's delight. They include: the original and ever-expanding Fairway, Citarella's fish and gourmet shop, H&H Bagels, and Zabar's deli. Conveniently, they all fall within a ten-block stretch. Residents are also grateful for the recent addition of more common grocery stores, such as a new Trader Joe's at 72nd Street and Broadway and Whole Foods and Michael's at 100th Street and Columbus.

What's missing in the Upper West Side?

The restaurants are often bland and underwhelming, and, while there are plenty cupcake bakeries, bread bakeries are sparse. Other than that, drawbacks are ones endemic in Manhattan – everything costs more than it should; getting "Junior" into a good public school is a full-time job, while private schools are expensive and wait-listed; the rat population never seems to wane, despite the city's repeated promises; and parking is a nightmare.   Nonetheless, most

Upper West Side residents wouldn't trade it for a Park Avenue penthouse.

ALPHABET CITY

Marc Andreo was educated at Brown University and the University of Chicago. He's been published in Pop Matters, E-How, About.com, and many other online publications.

Alphabet City

New York's Alphabet City has been a lively home to immigrants and bohemians over the decades. Located in Manhattan's Lower East Side, it gets its name from its location on Avenues A, B, C and D, above Houston Street and below 14th Street. In the mid-19th century, Alphabet City housed predominantly German immigrants and was even referred to as "Little Germany." Following, in the late-19th and early 20th centuries, it housed mostly Eastern European Jews, Irish and Italian immigrants.

Around the mid-1950s, Alphabet City began another demographic change as more Puerto Ricans began to settle there. The area slowly took on a distinctly Spanish flair and become known as "Loisaida" (Spanglish for "Lower East Side") to many of its residents. The name "Alphabet City" is thought to have been a fairly recent development, possibly established when the area became more gentrified, due to an influx of residents from the Village.

In recent decades the area has served as home to many bohemians and artists, alike. The area was on the cutting edge of the New York art scene—especially during the 1980s and early-1990s, as it housed many galleries, performance spaces, musicians, artists and poets. The bohemian scene was depicted in the hit musical "Rent," in which much of the action was set in Alphabet City. Under Mayor Giuliani in the early-1990s, the area became more gentrified, and crime rates dropped as a result. Soon, apartments were renovated and storefronts, cafes and nightlife began to spring up.

Today the Alphabet City area features a number of exciting restaurants, cafes, coffee shops, theaters and thrift stores, while also maintaining a distinctly Puerto Rican vibe. It is less gentrified than the East Village, and, though it may not be the artist's haven it once was, it's probably one of the most diverse sections of Manhattan. Artists, students, Puerto Ricans, Israelis and Dominicans dominate its demographics.

Currently, Alphabet City is generally a calm neighborhood, with a strong local identity. There are plenty of old punks, living in rent-controlled apartments, who have interesting, non-conformist political views as well as an array of Puerto Rican and Dominican families and a population of indie hipsters, strumming their guitars and skateboarding through the park. The area's streets and pre-war, low-rise apartments are currently undergoing some renovation (a heated subject amongst those who have lived in the neighborhood since the 1970s and 1980s because of the resulting increase in rent).

Many art and music festivals occur in the neighborhood's beautiful Tompkin's Square Park, which is bound by 7th and 8th Streets, between Avenues A and B. Tompkin's Square Park also hosts a weekly farmer's market, where local vendors from all across New York sell fresh vegetables, fruit, meats and other items.

Restaurants, Shopping and Nightlife

No one ever has a problem finding a place to eat in Alphabet City. There are many gourmet options, as well as local Israeli, Italian and Puerto Rican restaurants. Il Posto Accanto combines gourmet with a distinct, local feel and serves grilled calamari and fresh handmade pasta daily. Vegetarians and vegans will find plenty to rave about at Back Forty, on 12th Street and Avenue B, where they serve chilled summer soups, hearty winter vegan dishes and tempura-fried vegetables. Authentic Puerto Rican cuisine can be found at Casa Adela, a local hole-in-the-wall restaurant with plenty of character and well-seasoned, wholesome food. There are also a number of other local Puerto Rican and Dominican dive restaurants, as well as great falafel at Caffe Rakka, Rumi Café and Hummus Place.

Alphabet City also has an active nightlife amongst its many bars and clubs. Located on Houston and Avenue A, Stay features 1960's retro décor and a diverse mix of tunes. Eastern Bloc is the most popular gay club and has recently been visited by Madonna and other pop-culture celebrities. The area was conveniently constructed for pub crawls, with at least thirty bars in the neighborhood. The most active bars lie on Avenue A. Alphabet Lounge and Uncle Ming's are always packed on the weekends with rock-a-billy types, indie hipsters and young professionals seeking a glimpse of Alphabet City's distinct Bohemian atmosphere.

There are plenty of vintage stores and thrift shops between Avenue A and 1st Avenue on 8th and 9th Streets. A neighborhood favorite is Fabulous Fanny's, which sells vintage goods and clothing, as well as custom vintage glass frames.

Parks

Tompkin's Square Park provides Alphabet City with a relaxed, community hub. During the warmer months, the park will usually be packed with New Yorkers enjoying their meals on park benches, chatting, reading newspapers, feeding squirrels and listening to local street musicians. Ever since the art scene of the 1980s and the Tompkin's Square Riots of 1988, the park has been known for its alternative edge. Thus, many skateboarders, students and anarchists are frequent visitors.

The other major park in Alphabet City is the East River Park. The entrance lies on East 12th Street, and the park stretches along the East River, encompassing over 55 acres of land. Many athletes take advantage of its baseball and soccer fields, tennis courts, running track and bike paths.

Coffee Shops

Over the past decade, due to the influx of young creative professionals, several coffee shops have sprouted up all over Alphabet City. Many of the cafés are equipped with wifi and are frequented by locals. Ninth Street Espresso probably serves the best espresso—they take their espresso craft very seriously. Meanwhile, Ost Café's ambience attracts young creative professional designers. Café Pick Me Up is a local coffee house, where common conversation topics include art and politics. They also serve great salads and sandwiches. The Israeli-run B-Cup Café has couches for lounging and provides a more homey-feel than the other cafes in the neighborhood.

Transportation

It's not difficult to get to Alphabet City. The area is accessible by the L Train, only a block from the 1st Avenue stop. It is also accessible via the JMZ-FV Delancey and Essex stop. The neighborhood is small. In fact, the perimeter can be walked in a little over an hour.

Closing Thoughts

Alphabet City is one of the most diverse and vibrant communities in New York City. It's not only a great place for a quick lunch or coffee, but it's also a great, culturally diverse place to live. It's steeped in local politics and gentrification concerns and yet continues to maintain its Puerto Rican and bohemian identity.

Chinatown

Lenny Lubitz is a native New Yorker who has lived in a number of neighborhoods in and around New York City though Chinatown will always hold a special place in his heart. An erstwhile itinerant and graduate student, his travels range from the Middle East to the Far East, as he lives by the creed that "everyplace I put my head down is home."

The Good News

1. Hong Kong without the jet lag.
New York's Chinatown is not some Disneyesque reproduction of what China might look like...this is the real thing. A dynamic and vibrant neighborhood that doesn't seem authentic---it is the real deal!

2. Amazing deals.
Chinatown is full of amazing deals. Food is at the top of the list, with affordable foods ranging from street vendors to tablecloth restaurants...but it does not end there! Everything from neckties at 5 for $10 to great and inexpensive kitchenware to t-shirts that are so cheap that you will never need to do laundry, this is a shopper's paradise.

3. A aeighborhood that never sleeps.
Whether it is 3pm or 3am, Chinatown is a place you can always find a place to eat, a place to drink, and a karaoke bar to practice your American Idol audition!

The Bad News

1. Parking.
Parking is a bit of a commodity in Chinatown. Few legal spots exist, and many of these have been commandeered by the on duty (and off duty?) police who work in the neighborhood precinct, as well as the city jail which borders the neighborhood.

2. Menus in Chinese.
Many of the smaller restaurants hang their daily specials on placards hanging from the wall---written in Chinese. While most of the same information is available on the English menus, many visitors leave thinking that the more exotic dishes (which they would never order if they knew what they were) are being kept a secret from them.

3. There are two McDonalds.
It is a bit disconcerting to see the 'golden arches,' as it can ruin the feeling that you are walking along the streets of Hong Kong...unless you have been to the former British colony, in which case you are already used to this ubiquitous eatery.

Chinatown

New York's Lower East Side has been a haven to a collection of immigrant communities for almost two centuries. Most notable is Chinatown, a name used with pride by tens of thousands of Chinese residents of the neighborhood. Its borders are nominally defined as: Broadway on its western perimeter, Grand Street on its north, Worth Street on its south and Montgomery Street on its eastern edge. However, the truth is that Chinatown has been rapidly engulfing portions of Little Italy and Tribeca. But more to the point, Chinatown is a vibrant neighborhood which has more in common with Hong Kong than it does with almost any other part of New York City.

The Scene

For over a century, Mott Street between Canal Street and Chatham Square has been the epicenter of Chinatown. (**Quick Fact**: It is a only a few short strides from the infamous Five Points intersection that was the sight of the notorious crime capitol of the world during the mid 1800s-- made famous in the film "Gangs of New York.") Here, generations of immigrants from China's Canton province found a home, where they could find apartments, jobs, doctors, social services and every other necessity for survival without needing to learn English. In the past fifteen years, a second cluster has developed on East Broadway, just several blocks east. The newest wave of Chinese immigrants are from Fujian, a province where they speak Foochow rather than Cantonese. Both dialects are not mutually intelligible.

While Chinatown is famous for its vast array of restaurants and counterfeit luxury goods, it is also the home to dozens of banks, far more grocery markets and souvenir shops, diamond and jewelry stores, and a remarkable amount of hair salons (recently discovered by the women of Midtown as the greatest coiffure bargain ever to be found in America). Like Hong Kong, custom tailors will create fashionable suits to order, and price haggling between vendors and customers creates a frenzy of energy along the streets.

Housing

Housing in Chinatown is primarily made up of four and five story walkups with an occasional new condominium rising from the site of a former Laundromat, grocery store or parking lot. The new condos are priced as high as several million dollars, and the apartments in older buildings are virtually unattainable, partially due to rent stabilization regulations that make them too affordable for most tenants to leave. While the new buildings offer perfectly normal living environments, many of the rundown multifamily houses have far more residents than a small village. This is due to the fact that so many are illegally subdivided into rooming houses. Numerous bunk beds are crammed in, and its residents, consisting primarily of single Chinese laborers, work insane hours and come home for a few hours each morning or night for a little sleep.

Day to Day

Life in Chinatown can best be described as a cacophony. Sounds range from the chatter of conversations day and night (far louder around East Broadway because the cultural norm of Fujian is to speak as if you are verbally attacking each other) to the sounds of cars and trucks well into the night. The streets are narrow, causing all noise to echo in the urban canyons of brick and asphalt. However, this is part of the charm of the community.

Restaurants

Great food is available all day, and, while a bit mediocre late at night, a decent meal can be had until dawn. For lunch, "dim sum" is the best way to experience the incredible variety of Cantonese dishes available. Jin Fong (located on the second floor of 20 Elizabeth Street), which seats over 1,000 people, and Golden Bridge (also on the second floor of 50 Bowery), which holds 650 people, are the best locales for this feast. Small groups are seated at large round tables and joined by other diners. One can choose from dozens of different small dishes, each holding four or five dumplings, shrimp or other delicacies. Each dish costs just a few dollars, allowing a small group of people the opportunity to taste a number of different dishes at a minimal price. Other options include Vietnamese restaurants such as Cong Ly (124 Hester Street), whose rough décor belies the amazing pho (noodle soup) that makes it a popular destination, as well as Paris Sandwich (two locations but stick to 213 Grand Street), where the bánh mi (Vietnam's superior answer to the Cuban sandwich) are great! For dinner, Big Wong (67 Mott Street) offers traditional Cantonese fare for very reasonable prices, while Green Bo (66 Bayard Street) serves Shanghai-style dishes. Oriental Garden (14 Elizabeth Street) has the freshest seafood, proven by its sparking tanks in which dinner swims. For a late night meal, Wo Hop (17 Mott Street) is open all night long. It is not gourmet food, but always hot and fast and is another true Chinatown joint to experience. And not to be missed is the nightspot Apothéke. Reminiscent of a speakeasy, it can "easily" be located by the sign over its doorway left by the former tenant, the OK Gold Flower Restaurant at 9 Doyers Street.

Transportation

While some residents consider Chinatown as remote as Hong Kong harbor, it is in fact easier to reach than Times Square. Every major subway line reaches this neighborhood, and both uptown and downtown buses also stop there. Ironically, taxis are never anywhere to be found, compelling people to either take public transit or walk toward Wall Street or the Village, where yellow cabs begin to appear.

Most significantly defining Chinatown is its energy. This is a neighborhood that truly never closes. With 65 percent of its residents being between 18 and 64, it is a vibrant community. Seven days a week, all hours of the day and night, shops can be found doing business, and restaurants that serve locals and tourists alike make this one of New York's most dynamic neighborhoods.

Editor's Note: After publication The Golden Bridge closed. The author suggests The Golden Unicorn is a worthy substitute.

Cobble Hill

Leila Cohan-Miccio is a New York-based comedy and lifestyle writer. She is the co-creator/writer of *Vag Magazine*, a web comedy that goes behind the scenes of a hipster third-wave feminist magazine. *Vag Magazine* has been written up everywhere from *Salon* to the *New YorkObserver*. Leila also wrote the sketch show *This Is About Smith*, which recently enjoyed a six month run at New York's Upright Citizens Brigade Theatre. She is proud to be a current member of UCB Maude team Stone Cold Fox and has written twenty shows with former Maude team High Treason. Leila started studying at UCB in 2007 and has worked with teachers like Neil Casey and Joe Wengert. She is now a teacher herself.

As a lifestyle writer, Leila's work has appeared in the *New York Magazine*-owned property Grub Street (the Boston edition of which she wrote and edited for three years), T*he Vogue City*, and *Carroll Gardens and Park Slope Patch*, for which she serves as restaurant critic. She is a proud Smith alum, a wicked Masshole, and better than you at Jeopardy. You can learn more about the things she likes (mostly baby animals and musical theater) at *www.leilacohanmiccio.com*.

The Good News

1. Aesthetics.

Cobble Hill is truly one of Brooklyn's prettiest neighborhoods. The streets are lined with trees, the brownstones are cozy and classic, and even the shops tend to have retro-style picturesque awnings.

2. Shopping.

From upscale women's boutiques like Teddy and Neda to paper shops like Papel New York, Cobble Hill's commercial district offers a plethora of cute, locally-owned shopping options.

3. Nightlife.

Sure, you don't come to Cobble Hill for a wild night, but the neighborhood offers a great diversity of drinking options: craft cocktails at Clover Club, giant beer selection at Strong Place, wine aplenty at Sample. Bonus: unlike in Manhattan or Williamsburg, you can almost always get a seat.

The Bad News

1. Snow nightmare .
Due to its narrow streets and New York municipal inefficiencies, Cobble Hill is often one of New York's last neighborhoods to get plowed when it snows. During a recent blizzard, some streets waited more than 60 hours to get service.

2. Expensive.
All those pretty aesthetics don't come cheap. From rent to shopping, living in Cobble Hill will cost you.

3. All babies, all the time.
If you don't like having your coffee shop writing time, brunch, or even after work drinks interrupted by rambunctious toddlers, Cobble Hill might not be for you.

Cobble Hill

Moms with triple-wide strollers mingle with elderly Italian immigrants while perusing pork belly at some of the city's best butcher shops. Taquerias are nestled next to craft cocktail bars on well-maintained streets full of historical brownstones. It is just another day in Cobble Hill, a Brooklyn, New York neighborhood that offers a little something for everyone.

Cobble Hill's boundaries are generally considered to be Atlantic Avenue to the north, Degraw Street to the south, Smith Street to the east and Hicks Street to the west. Most of the neighborhood's commercial activity is focused along Smith, Court and Atlantic, though there are thriving businesses along Henry and Clinton Streets as well. Cobble Hill is bordered by Brooklyn Heights to the north, Carroll Gardens to the south, Boerum Hill to the east and Red Hook to the west. Though frequently mentioned in the same breath as Boerum Hill and Carroll Gardens (the three areas are sometimes referred to by the name Bococa), Cobble Hill has its own distinct identity.

Cobble Hill was used as a fort during both the Revolutionary War and the War of 1812, but, these days, tourists to the neighborhood are much more likely to be gawking at streets seen in recent movies and television shows than military history. In the past five years alone, Spiderman 3, Eat, Pray, Love, and The Real Housewives of New York City have all been filmed along Cobble Hill's tree-filled streets. Perhaps unsurprisingly, given the neighborhood's cinematic prominence, Cobble Hill boasts several celebrity residents, including Norah Jones, Lili Taylor and Ween frontman Aaron Freeman (also known as Gene Ween).

Housing

Most of Cobble Hill's housing is in the form of Italianate-style brownstones. Though some are single-family houses, the majority are split into apartments, with each apartment generally occupying a full floor. Low-rise apartment buildings are interspersed with the brownstones, particularly along Court and Smith Streets. The majority of Cobble Hill residents rent their apartments. While prices are lower than Manhattan, they are higher than most of Brooklyn, with studios running over $1,200, and other apartments are at least $800-$1,000 per bedroom. Sale prices are high; a brownstone will typically go for well over one million dollars.

Restaurants

Smith Street is widely considered to be southern Brooklyn's major restaurant row. The food options are diverse, with everything from sushi to barbecue available in a nine block stretch. Some of the best options include: the Michelin Guide-recommended Saul (140 Smith Street), which offers upscale New American fare like seared foie gras with poached rhubarb, the bacon and bourbon-focused Char No. 4 (196 Smith Street) and casual Italian spot Lunetta (116 Smith Street), where the carbonara is to die for. Court Street's restaurants are more old-school. At Sam's Italian Cuisine (238 Court Street) the decor is minimal; the drink list is fifty years old; and the pizzas are giant and delicious. A third restaurant row is quietly growing along the northern end of Henry Street, with classic American food at Henry Public (329 Henry Street), delicate Japanese fare at Hibino (333 Henry Street) and Italian sandwiches and small plates at Bocca Lupo (391 Henry Street). Most restaurants in the neighborhood offer delivery.

Nightlife

Cobble Hill's drinking options are as legion as the neighborhood's restaurants, with something to suit almost every mood. Looking for a laid-back beer bar? Drop by Boat (175 Smith Street). Craving artisanal cocktails made with specially-shaped ice cubes and craft spirits? Don't miss Clover Club (210 Smith Street). Sample (152 Smith Street) is probably one of the city's best kept secrets. It is a cozy Spanish-themed bar with super-cheap, super-strong cocktails and a great backyard. Bonus: Cobble Hill's bars are almost always less crowded than Manhattan's.

Shopping

While Cobble Hill definitely isn't the best place to come for cheap clothes (or cheap anything, really), if one has some money to throw around, the neighborhood features a wealth of shopping options. Bird (220 Smith Street) and Teddy (216 Court Street) offer high-end women's clothing, and Epaulet (231 Smith Street) offers a nice selection of clothing and shoes for men. BookCourt (163 Court Street) is one of the borough's largest book stores. Cobble Hill's shopping, however, shines brightest in the area of food. Los Paisanos (162 Smith Street) caters to the neighborhood's Italian immigrant population, but residents of all stripes enjoy the ample selection of well-priced high-quality meats. Stinky (261 Smith Street) offers a plethora of cured meats and cheeses, and sister store Smith and Vine (268 Smith Street) sells the wine to go with them. The neighborhood's more budget-minded residents are also grateful for the presence of Brooklyn's only Trader Joe's (130 Court Street). Unfortunately, lines on the weekend can be astronomical.

Transportation

Though Cobble Hill is located just a short distance from Manhattan, transportation options are not ideal. The neighborhood is served by the F and G trains at Bergen, but both lines suffer from frequent delays and re-routing. Sadly, most bus service to Cobble Hill was eliminated in the MTA's

June 2010 service cuts. Here's the good news: it's just a short walk from Cobble Hill to Brooklyn Heights' Borough Hall station, where one can catch the 2, 3, 4, 5 and R trains.

Demographics

Cobble Hill's residents are largely split between the Italian families, who own many of the neighborhood's brownstones and the young urban professionals, who rent from them. The neighborhood is chockablock with young families. Coffee shops like Cafe Pedlar (210 Court Street) get awfully noisy right before toddler nap time, and it's rare to pass a storefront without at least one dog tied to a post in front.

Though there are drawbacks to living in Cobble Hill (it's certainly not cheap and the transportation options could be improved), residents seem to be willing to put up with the inconvenience.

Carroll Gardens

Leila Cohan-Miccio is a New York-based comedy and lifestyle writer. She is the co-creator/writer of Vag Magazine, a web comedy that goes behind the scenes of a hipster third-wave feminist magazine. Vag Magazine has been written up everywhere from Salon to the New York Observer. Leila also wrote the sketch show This Is About Smith, which recently enjoyed a six month run at New York's Upright Citizens Brigade Theatre. She is proud to be a current member of UCB Maude team Stone Cold Fox and have written twenty shows with former Maude team High Treason. Leila started studying at UCB in 2007 and has worked with teachers like Neil Casey and Joe Wengert. She is now a teacher herself.

As a lifestyle writer, Leila's work has appeared in the New York Magazine-owned property Grub Street (the Boston edition of which she wrote and edited for three years), The Vogue City, and Carroll Gardens and Park Slope Patch, for which she serves as restaurant critic. She is a proud Smith alum, a wicked Masshole, and better than you at Jeopardy. You can learn more about the things she likes (mostly baby animals and musical theater) at www.leilacohanmiccio.com.

The Good News

1. *Restaurants.*
From Frankies 457 Spuntino and Prime Meats to Buttermilk Channel, Carroll Gardens is on the frontlines of the New Brooklyn restaurant movement: a culinary philosophy emphasizing top-notch ingredients and simple preparations.

2. *Friendliness.*
Carroll Gardens residents can frequently be found chatting with each other, whether on their stoops or in the aisles of local grocery stores. It's a real community - a rare find in New York.

3. *Food shopping.*
If you like cooking Italian food, you'll love Carroll Gardens. From G. Esposito and Sons Pork Store to the fresh pasta at Caputo's, Carroll Gardens is a gastronomic dream.

The Bad News

1. *Subway access*.
Carroll Gardens is served exclusively by the F and G trains. The G doesn't go to Manhattan (and on weekends, frequently doesn't go at all), and the F is riddled by service issues.

2. *Sleepy*.
Though Carroll Gardens offers some excellent drinking options (see: cocktails at Brooklyn Social and beer at Bar Great Harry), even the main streets are near-abandoned after midnight.

3. *Lack of diversity*.
Carroll Gardens is almost exclusively comprised of Italian families and young, mostly white professionals. This is not a great example of New York's famous melting pot.

Carroll Gardens

Hipsters play board games and down $6 Pimm's Cups at a neighborhood bar, while, around the corner, parents tend to their spacious gardens and teenagers socialize on brownstone stoops. Celebrities pop into one of New York's pizzerias, bumping into Italian-speaking old-timers on their way out. All of that, and so much more, can be found in the leafy streets of Carroll Gardens.

Carroll Gardens' boundaries are generally considered to be Degraw Street to the north, Hamilton Avenue to the south, Hoyt Street to the east and Hicks Street to the west. Most of the neighborhood's commercial activity is focused along Smith and Court Streets, though there are thriving businesses along Henry Street as well. Carroll Gardens is bordered by Cobble Hill to the north, Boerum Hill to the east and Red Hook to the south and west.

Demographics

Carroll Gardens' name comes jointly from Declaration of Independence signer, Charles Carroll, and the massive gardens in front of many of the neighborhood's houses. Although the neighborhood was originally occupied by, mostly, Irish immigrants, many Italian immigrants moved in during the 1900s. The Italian population still owns many of the buildings, and the apartments are rented by young professionals.

Housing

Most of Carroll Gardens' residents live in Italianate-style brownstones. Though there are some single-family homes, the majority of the brownstones are split into apartments, with each apartment usually occupying an entire floor. Along Smith and Court Streets (as well as 1st through 4th Places), low-rise apartment buildings are also common. Most Carroll Gardens' residents are renters and prices aren't cheap; studios start around $1,000 and, though better deals can be found, renters can generally expect to pay between $700 and $1,100 per bedroom. Sale prices are also high, with brownstones costing at least one million dollars.

Food and Drink

Carroll Gardens offers some of Brooklyn's best dining options and, whether you're craving pizza or soul food, there's probably something to sate your craving. Unlike in the neighboring Cobble Hill, Court Street, not Smith Street, is the biggest restaurant row. Buttermilk Channel (524 Court Street) serves up wildly popular seasonal American fare (don't miss the linguine with Brussels sprouts, mushrooms and breadcrumbs). The rustic Italian fare at Frankies 457 Spuntino (457 Court Street) has a major cult following (word to the wise: brunch is less crowded than dinner and includes New York's best French toast). Lucali (575 Henry Street) offers near-perfect pizzas and is reported to be Jay-Z and Beyonce's favorite spot for a date. The Brooklyn Farmacy (513 Henry Street) is modeled after an old-time soda shop and serves up killer ice cream sundaes and sodas. Most restaurants in the neighborhood offer takeout and delivery.

Carroll Gardens' bar selection isn't quite as extensive as that of Cobble Hill, but the boozing options are still nothing to sneer at. Abilene (442 Court Street), a neighborhood bar worth traveling for, boasts ultra-cheap cocktails and board games. Black Mountain Wine House (415 Union Street) offers an extensive wine selection in an extraordinarily cozy room, and Brooklyn Social (335 Smith Street) has a killer cocktail list.

Shopping

Carroll Gardens' shopping scene is small but worthwhile. G. Esposito & Sons Pork Store (357 Court Street) is a neighborhood institution, offering screamingly fresh meat and Italian prepared foods at exceptionally reasonable prices. D'Amico Foods (309 Court Street) roasts and grinds their own coffee on the premises (don't miss the complex and nutty Red Hook Blend). The staff at Scotto's Wine Cellar (318 Court Street) keeps track of customers' likes and dislikes and offers a good selection of liquor in addition to wine. Olive's Very Vintage (434 Court Street) boasts a substantial selection of vintage duds, complete with some excellent bargains.

Transportation

Transportation options are far and away the biggest drawback to living in Carroll Gardens. The neighborhood is served by the F and G trains at Carroll Street and Smith/9th Street, but both lines suffer from frequent delays and re-routing. Sadly, most bus service to Carroll Gardens was eliminated in the Metropolitan Transportation Authority's June 2010 service cuts.

Parks and Recreation

Though Carroll Gardens doesn't boast the park space of, say, Park Slope, Carroll Park, located on Carroll Street between Smith and Court, is quite pleasant for a small green space. There is a good-sized playground that is, typically, teeming with the neighborhood's substantial small fry population as well as sprinklers and, as an acknowledgement of the area's still-substantial Italian population, well-maintained bocce courts.

Carroll Gardens might not have the active nightlife of Manhattan, the convenience of Brooklyn Heights or the trendiness of Williamsburg, but most of the neighborhood's residents, drawn in by the killer restaurants, beautiful streetscapes and friendly atmosphere, wouldn't change a thing.

Bay Ridge

Lauren McGrail currently resides in Park Slope, Brooklyn where she is an avid lover of food, drinks, laughter, and good times. She is a writer and filmmaker currently working on producing her first feature film, which she also wrote. Lauren is also a blogger and frequent twitterbug.

The Good News

1. With its residential feel, it's a great place for children and families. It's like a small town with the convenience of a subway to the city.

2. Several great restaurants that are worth traveling for within walking distance. Especially The Kettle Black, which surely has the best wings in Brooklyn.

3. The pier off of Shore Road, with fantastic views of Manhattan and fresh sea air, is a hidden gem.

The Bad News

1. With the R as the only train option, the commute to Manhattan and even other parts of Brooklyn can be quite lengthy, especially on the weekend, when the R train is occasionally out of service and replaced by shuttle busses.

2. While there are great restaurants in the neighborhood, the best of them tend to be pricy.

3. A Restaurants, while great in quality, can lack in diversity.

Bay Ridge

A thirty-minute drive from Manhattan, Bay Ridge is located in the southwest corner of Brooklyn, New York. Its general space can be seen on a map as the area framed by the Shore Parkway and the Gowanus Expressway. Technically speaking, the borders of the neighborhood are 65th Street in the north, 101st Street in the south, the Shore Road in the west, and Interstate 278 in the east.

Bay Ridge was once called Yellow Hook, a name that was changed in the mid-1800s. As yellow fever struck the community and Brooklyn at large, the community of residents living in the area felt the name was insensitive. The Yellow Hook Grill on 3rd Avenue and Ovington Avenue is one of the few reminders of Bay Ridge's old name.

Demographics

The neighborhood has a distinctly familial feel, and many of the multigenerational families in Bay Ridge have had ties to the neighborhood for decades. Many of the business owners in the neighborhood also live there, so it's easy to recognize people after spending only a bit of time living and playing in Bay Ridge.

Largely a middle-class community, Bay Ridge has significant Arab, Italian, Irish and Greek populations. Historically Norwegian, Bay Ridge continues to be the site of the annual Norwegian-American parade, despite the shrinking of the Norwegian influence in the area.

Transportation

The R train is the only subway that services the neighborhood, with stops along 4th Avenue at Bay Ridge Avenue, 78th Street, 86th Street and 95th Street. If one is traveling from Bay Ridge to the busier areas of Manhattan, a switch to an Express D or N train at either 59th or 36th Streets in Brooklyn is a must, since the R is local and taking it all the way into the city is time consuming.

Bus travel is also widely used, though it is not uncommon for families living in the neighborhood to have at least one car. As a result, parking can be difficult to come by after seven or eight in the evening.

Shops and Nightlife

Most of the commerce in Bay Ridge can be found on 3rd and 5th Avenues, between Bay Ridge Avenue and 86th Street, with restaurants and boutiques as well as hair salons, hardware stores, dollar stores and bars lining both avenues. Although most of the boutiques, salons and stores close by 9 p.m. or so, the restaurants and bars in the neighborhood provide opportunities for a night out.

Fifth Avenue is the quieter of the two stretches, punctuated by a few memorable restaurants and peppered with many smaller takeout establishments along the way.   Schnitzel Haus on 73rd Street serves up authentic German fare and Agnati Meze on 78th Street is a destination for those seeking Greek food.

Skinflints on 79th Street is a true neighborhood bar. It has stained glass window treatments and lamps that provide wonderful ambience for the usual crowd of neighborhood residents. Come for the drinks and atmosphere at Skinflints, though, because the food will often leave something to be desired.

On 3rd Avenue, one will find a variety of dining experiences, including the Yellow Hook Grill, an American-style Bar and Grill, and Grandma's Pizzeria, an Italian eatery to the north. Walking south near 86th Street, one finds a variety of Italian restaurants, including Areo at 84th Street and Chianti at 85th Street.

Also on 3rd Avenue is The Salty Dog, a sports bar that caters to the large firefighter population in the neighborhood. The Salty Dog is crowded on any weekend night and many weekday nights.   The Kettle Black at 87th Street and 3rd Avenue is another popular drinking spot and serves some of the best chicken wings in Brooklyn. Moving further south on 3rd Avenue, one will find the upscale Cebu on 88th Street and Nouvelle on 87th Street, which serves inventive French/ Asian fusion.

For shopping in the neighborhood, 86th Street offers conveniences such as Century 21, a department store, and chain stores such as The Gap, New York and Company and Payless Shoes. Food City on 74th Street and 3rd Avenue and Associated on 3rd Avenue between 79th and 80th Streets are passable grocery spots. Both offer a limited variety and are small enough to make major grocery shopping frustrating on a crowded weekend or after work. The newly opened Key Food on Bay Ridge Avenue, just beyond 3rd Avenue, offers more space and variety. All close early, around 9 or 10 p.m., but the copious 24-hour bodegas in the area will generally have what one needs beyond 10 p.m.

Weekends

Bright summer weekend days will find many of the residents of Bay Ridge out and about. While walking west of 3rd Avenue, one will find an area of the neighborhood that feels completely removed from the city or even 3rd and 5th Avenues. This area is distinctly residential, and the interesting architecture makes getting lost on a meandering walk an interesting day out. Vast mansions spring up on streets that are otherwise home to typical brownstones. The famed Gingerbread House at 83rd Street and Narrows Avenue is one worthy of a diversion.

Those heading west of 3rd Avenue will find themselves pursuing the views of the waterfront on Shore Road. Parks in this area provide space for families, and the underpass at Bay Ridge Avenue and Shore Road provides an entrance to a pier and a walkway/bike path that stretches well beyond the Verrazano Bridge. Many come here to exercise and enjoy the spectacular view of the Manhattan skyline to the north.

In Bay Ridge, one could move from bustling city atmospheres to quiet residential streets to expansive parks and waterfront walks in one afternoon. For many residents, this distinctive mix of atmospheres and feelings is its charm. Many of the people who live there also exist there, which is an homage to all that Bay Ridge has to offer.

The neighborhood's array of restaurants and shops, along with its cordoned off and largely residential location, gives way to the feeling that one is in a small town rather than a neighborhood in the bustling borough of Brooklyn.

Park Slope

Lauren McGrail   Lauren currently resides in Park Slope, Brooklyn where she is an avid lover of food, drinks, laughter, and good times.   She is a writer and filmmaker currently working on producing her first feature film, which she also wrote. Lauren is also a blogger and frequent twitterbug.

The Good News

1. Some of the best restaurants and bars in Brooklyn are within easy walking distance.

2. With various train options, work commutes to other parts of Brooklyn or Manhattan are usually only between twenty and thirty minutes.

3. The neighborhood's vicinity to Prospect Park adds a great deal to the lifestyle here, especially in the spring, summer, and fall. Even when there aren't free concerts and events going on, the park is the place to be in the summer in Brooklyn and to be within walking distance to it is a great luxury to have.

The Bad News

1. The rumors are true: babies and dogs are copious here, and they occupy and create obstacles on most every sidewalk.

2. It can be hard to find good late night food. Most restaurants stop serving food around 11pm, so if you're heading back from drinks in Manhattan with friends, it's best to get food before returning home to Park Slope.

3. The rent is quite high. You're paying for vicinity to the park and great restaurants and access to a community - and trust me, you're paying a lot for it.

Park Slope

Park Slope is a large neighborhood in Brooklyn, New York. It's bordered by Flatbush Avenue to the north, 4th Avenue to the west, Prospect Park West to the east, and 15th Street to the south. However, with commerce growing in Park Slope South, some argue that the southern border of the neighborhood has become 20th or 22nd Street in recent years. It's known for its proximity to Prospect Park, and its wide brownstone-lined residential streets.

Housing

The majority of the commerce in this area occurs on 7th and 5th Avenues, and most residents live on the east to west streets between the two. The architecture is largely old and classic – brownstones line most of the wide, tree-lined streets. New architecture in recent years has brought large, modern luxury condo buildings, which vastly contrasts the more traditional brownstone look of the neighborhood.

Transportation

Transportation is copious in this area, and, depending on where one needs to be in the neighborhood, he or she can take the R, F, G, 1, 2 or 3 trains. However, due to budget cuts in 2010, much of the bus service in Park Slope has been cut.

Demographics

Visitors to Park Slope often take notice of the large population of strollers and dogs. Because the residents are mainly young families, often with two working parents, day care centers and dog walking services are popular in Park Slope.

In 2010, New York Magazine named Park Slope the best place to live in New York City.   Residents of the neighborhood are predominantly white and are largely wealthy upper-middle class people. According to the 2000 Census, residents here are seventy-seven percent white, eight percent African American, five percent Asian and ten percent Hispanic. Thirteen percent of the population is denoted as "other races," and one percent of the residents are two races.

Shopping and Dining Options

Park Slope is often referred to in two sections: North Park Slope, which generally refers to the area between Flatbush Avenue to the north and 9th Street to the south, and Park Slope South, which refers to the area south of 9th Street to approximately Prospect Avenue or a few blocks beyond.

North Park Slope is the busier of the two sections, with many restaurants, boutiques and bars. Although the residents of Park Slope certainly dine and shop here, this part of town is also often visited by people who do not live here due to its excellent selection of restaurants and shops.

The newly renovated Moutarde on 5th Avenue at Carroll Street offers delicious French fare, and one might satisfy a craving for fish and chips at Chip Shop on 5th Avenue at 6th Street. For other seafood dishes, one might visit Brooklyn Fish Camp, where nightly specials such as all-you-can-eat shrimp are supplemented by delicious side dishes like hush puppies. Brooklyn Fish Camp offers high-end dining in a low-key atmosphere.

Those looking to have a drink in North Slope might visit Loki. It has plenty of space with a typical bar setup in the front, a pool table in the middle, and couches for a lounge-feel in the back. Total Wine Bar serves up a completely satisfying and quiet night. The place has a distinctly familiar feel. It's easy to make friends while sitting at the bar, which wraps around the center where the bartenders pour wine.

Shopping in Park Slope predominantly focuses on small boutiques and gift shops. In recent years several vintage and consignment shops have popped up in North Slope, including Beacon's Closet on 5th Street and Warren and Odd Twin on 5th Street at Degraw.

Beyond 9th Street, where Park Slope becomes Park Slope South, the businesses have a quainter feel to them than those in North Park Slope. At Naidre's, a coffee shop with organic and vegan soup, salad and sandwich offerings, it's not uncommon for the staff to know at least half of the line by name. Grumpy Coffee is another hotspot, serving up coffee from around the globe that is freshly brewed by the cup. Don't expect to dawdle at Grumpy's, though – the space is small and laptops aren't allowed.

Park Slope South has several hidden gems for dining, many of which are frequented by residents of the area more than people who are visiting for a night out. Toby's on 6th Avenue and 20th Street combines a casual ambience with fine ingredients with brick oven pizzas that are too good not to finish. Bar Toto on 6th Avenue and 11th Street has a great ambience and always offers dependably delicious Italian fare, and Café Steinhoff at 14th Street and 7th Avenue serves some of the best Austrian food in Brooklyn.

Residents of Park Slope do a lot of their grocery shopping in the neighborhood, which offers several Key Foods locations. Union Market, a fine foods market, is often the easiest place to run for a thing or two because there are multiple locations in Park Slope. However, it will set you back more than a bodega or chain might. Many residents also belong to the Park Slope co-op on Union Street between 6th and 7th Avenues, an icon of the neighborhood.

Weekends

A weekend will find many residents of the area going for a stroll in the neighborhood followed by brunch at popular spots such as Miriam on 5th Avenue at Prospect Place or Dizzy's Diner on 9th Street at 8th Avenue. The wait at either might be up to thirty minutes.

In the summer, many will retreat to Prospect Park on long, hot afternoons for picnics large and small. In the summer, it's not uncommon to see as many as fifty people gathered for a barbecue in the park. *Celebrate Brooklyn!*, an annual music concert series in Prospect Park, brings crowds any night of the week with its free concerts from June to August.

Park Slope is a vast neighborhood with much to offer its residents and its visitors. With its shops, restaurants, bars, and its proximity to Prospect Park, one can easily spend an entire day doing nothing but exploring Park Slope.

Prospect Heights

Fahmida Y Rashid has lived in big cities all her life, and thrives on convenience and busy vibes. Having grown up in Tokyo and New York City, crowds aren't a problem, and she doesn't know what it's like to have to mow a lawn. She's bounced around several neighborhoods in New York City before settling down in Brooklyn. A technology and travel writer during the week, she spends her weekends down by the bay. However, her heart is down in Coney Island munching on a Nathan's hot dog during the summer.

The Good News

1. *Numerous Cultural Attractions.*
Culture is only steps away, such as the varied exhibits at Brooklyn Museum, concerts and films at the Brooklyn Academy of Music, and the botanist's paradise at the Brooklyn Botanical Garden. Prospect Park is a great meeting spot with friends as well as to unwind.

2. *Relatively Affordable.*
For anyone working in Manhattan, the amount of time it takes to get in to work is very important. Prospect Heights has the benefit of being close, without the high prices plaguing Park Slope, Boerum Hill and Cobble Hill. Not being fully-gentrified has its benefits. While other Brooklyn neighborhoods are cheaper, the short commuting time makes the prices palatable.

3. *Diverse*
The neighborhood is truly culturally diverse, with Caribbean immigrants living alongside lont-time Italian and German residents. There are all types of ethnic cuisine available, and the entire neighborhood gets some island pride for the West Indian Day Parade over Labor Day weekend.

The Bad News

1. Not yet fully-gentrified.
There is still a bit of a rough vibe in several of the neighborhoods. Alongside the new luxury high-rise buildings are rundown brownstones, and some areas are more family-friendly than others.

2. Not car friendly.
Washington, Vanderbilt and Flatbush Avenues are all very busy streets, as is Eastern Parkway. Along with the ars clogging up the main shopping arteries, street parking is also notoriously hard to find at any time.

3. Too close to Atlantic Yards.
Prospect Heights is immediately south of where Bruce Rather is putting up his controversial Atlantic Yards development. Along with the arena for the Brooklyn Nets basketball team, the complex will include high-rise condos. It is expected to add to the traffic problem (see above) and change the entire feel of the neighborhood.

Prospect Heights

Only 20 minutes by subway from midtown Manhattan, Prospect Heights was once a "forgotten" neighborhood; no one looked twice at the quiet, tree-lined, working-class neighborhood. In recent years, this tiny trapezoid-shaped area has transformed from a run-down, blue-collar community into a well-established, middle-class nabe.

Lying between Park Slope, Fort Greene and Crown Heights, Prospect Heights is traditionally defined by Flatbush Avenue to the west, Atlantic Avenue to the north, Eastern Parkway to the south, and Washington Avenue to the east. Brooklyn borders are notoriously fluid, and many people claim Franklin Avenue, a half mile further, as the eastern border. The controversial Atlantic Yards project is right on Atlantic Avenue, as well. Atlantic Yards will eventually be an enormous mixed-use commercial/residential development and home to the NBA's Nets franchise.

Attractions

Prospect Heights is home to some of the best cultural institutions in Brooklyn, including the Brooklyn Museum, the central branch of the Brooklyn Public Library, the Brooklyn Botanical Garden, the Brooklyn Academy of Music and the 585-acre urban oasis called "Prospect Park."

With a 60-acre lake, a forest, a zoo and other attractions, Prospect Park is bustling with things to do every day. Many also forego the attractions and simply enjoy picnics on the Long Meadow.

Shops and Restaurants

There are four main commercial arteries running through the neighborhood -- Underhill, Flatbush, Vanderbilt and Washington avenues. Chain stores, such as American Apparel, have invaded Flatbush Avenue, but bars, restaurants, specialized boutiques and mom-and-pop stores still dominate local business.

Some local restaurants are well-known, with diners converging from all five boroughs. Tom's Restaurant, a mom-and-pop diner on Washington Avenue and Sterling Place, is one. If there is a line for a table, the staff hands out free coffee, oranges and cookies to ease the wait. The food is basic, but delicious diner fare. It's a great place to get a homemade Cherry-Lime Rickey.

Beast, on Bergen Street and Vanderbilt Avenue, is another. The Spanish tapas are larger than anything served in Spain and feature potatoes, chorizo, a wide range of seafood and creamy Spanish cheeses. The weekend brunch menu has a decidedly Spanish flair (chipotle pepper Hollandaise?).

Demographics

Prospect Heights' residents are a diverse mix of races and income groups. From the 1910s to 1950s, the neighborhood was primarily Italian, Jewish and German. Since then, other nationalities -- both new immigrants and New Yorkers looking for affordable housing -- have moved in. Reflecting the heavy concentration of Caribbean immigrants in the area, the city's largest annual parade, the West Indian Day Parade, winds its way along Eastern Parkway and concludes at Grand Army Plaza every Labor Day. Over two million visitors regularly turn out for the parade each year.

Even though the majority of the residents are African-American, in recent years, the newcomers have tended to be white, college-educated and well-off. Prospect Heights' residents are generally couples in their late-twenties. Even though there are many families -- many of whom were priced out of Park Slope- - living in Prospect Heights, the neighborhood doesn't exactly have a family-friendly vibe.

Housing and Architecture

Though graced with lovely turn-of-the-century, three-story brownstones and elegant 1920's apartment buildings, the neighborhood has also seen a significant amount of development, including new offices, luxury high-rise condominiums and low-and-moderate-income co-ops. Sometimes, the architecture is visually jarring, with older homes juxtaposed with condos in gleaming structures of glass and steel.

The majority of available housing options are two- or three-bedroom rentals; although, there is a brisk market for houses, condos and co-ops. The median rent is about $1,000 for a one-bedroom, but $1,500 studios aren't unheard of. There are plenty of two- and three- family homes available for rent, but most renters end up choosing apartment buildings with 20 units or more. The majority of the houses, condos and co-ops are two-bedroom properties.

The city designated much of the area as a historic district because of the heavy concentration of Neo-Grec row houses and brownstones. The Prospect Heights Historic District is bounded by Flatbush, Sterling, Washington and St. Marks avenues. The Prospect Heights Neighborhood Development Council often runs house tours in October as a fund-raiser. While the enclave (fifth largest in the city) is beautiful and serene, the designation can be problematic for property owners. For example, the extra regulations make property maintenance expensive, since the building facade has to remain consistent with the neighbors'.

Transportation

The area is well-served by public transportation. The D, Q, 2, 3, 4 or 5 subway lines cut right through the neighborhood, and it is a quick hop into Manhattan or deeper into Brooklyn, such as Flatbush or Coney Island. It's walking-friendly because Prospect Heights covers less than a quarter of a square mile and the streets are on a grid. Several bus lines connect Prospect Heights to the rest of Brooklyn, such as the B41, B45, B65 and B69. The B49 and B44 buses are a few short blocks away in Crown Heights.

Schools

Many Prospect Heights children attend Teunis G Bergen School (P.S. 9) and Bergen Upper School (M.S. 571), both housed in the same building on Underhill Avenue. PS 9 did not have a good reputation within the community a decade ago, but a heavily involved Parent Teacher Association, proactive principal and dedicated teachers changed that. The school emphasizes small classrooms and extra additions to the standard curriculum. MS 571 is not as well regarded still, as students are barely getting by. There are four small high schools, each with a unique focus: Brooklyn School for Music and Theater, Brooklyn Academy for Science and the Environment, International High School at Prospect Heights and the High School for Global Citizenship. The high schools have metal detectors. Acorn Community High School is right on the border with Crown Heights.

Prospect Heights benefits from its close proximity to everything, including Manhattan, trendy Brooklyn hotspots and natural and cultural attractions. Plus, relatively speaking, it is cheaper than many other up-and-coming Brooklyn neighborhoods.

Hamilton Heights

Jordan Rubenstein is a human rights advocate and freelance writer. She currently works at Congregation Beit Simchat Torah, the world's largest lesbian, gay, bisexual, and transgender (LGBT) synagogue. As a writer for Change.org and Next Magazine, she spends much of her free time advocating for human rights. Jordan eagerly moved to New York City after graduating from Carnegie Mellon University in Pittsburgh.

The Good News

1. Great Housing.
While you may think it's impossible to find an inexpensive apartment in Manhattan that's also spacious, unique, and attractive on the inside and outside...apartments in Hamilton Heights have it all. They are also much more reasonable than other areas and it's easy to find a nice apartment with plenty of character.

2. Aesthetics.
Hamilton Heights has both beautiful, tree-lined streets with nice apartment buildings as well as long stretches of quiet parks for a relaxing walk. The neighborhood is charming and attractive.

3. Diversity.
Residents of Hamilton Heights span all ages and races. Walking around the neighborhood, you're bound to hear people speak in a variety of languages. Large families live in the same apartment buildings as students, and on a trip to the local laundromat, you'll see New York City's melting pot first-hand.

The Bad News

1. Dining Options.
While there are countless fast food chains, delis, and small grocery stores in Hamilton Heights, there are few good, sit-down restaurants. While it's nice to have the choice between Taco Bell, McDonald's, and Burger King, it would be nice to have some better options too.

2. Lack of Nightlife.
If you're planning to go to a lot of bars and clubs, you'll end up spending much of your time elsewhere. Hamilton Heights has a few bars, but there isn't a very vibrant nightlife. If you're up past midnight and want to wander the neighborhood, you won't have places to go other than 24 hour delis and fast food chains.

3. Distance.
While Hamilton Heights is easily accessible by the subway, it's far away from Midtown and Downtown. Prepare to get a monthly Metrocard because walking to your evening activities likely won't be an option. When the subway is running smoothly it only takes 20 minutes to get to Midtown by subway -- but if the subway isn't functioning, your social life won't be functioning either.

Hamilton Heights

Hamilton Heights is an interesting place to live, rich with the diversity of various cultures. The neighborhood has a great community spirit and no shortage of activity. But what sets it apart from other neighborhoods in Manhattan is that the area is beautiful -- parks are abundant, trees line many of the streets, and several of the apartment buildings were designed by notable architects.

Housing

Hamilton Heights is a desirable place to live for those looking for affordable, beautiful housing. The neighborhood is home to tree-lined streets with elegant-looking brownstones. The architecture is unique and varied, offering many wonderful choices for attractive housing. Recent construction and large housing developments offer additional housing in Hamilton Heights, although these buildings don't share the same architectural appeal as the small, row houses.

Demographics

Hamilton Heights is both culturally and historically significant. It was named after Alexander Hamilton, who lived in the area for the last two years of his life in the early

1800s, when the area was still mostly farmland. The neighborhood was initially composed of middle-class families and individuals. Many were born in the United States, and the immigrant populations were mostly from Germany, Ireland and Italy. Famous residents included Norman Rockwell, Oscar Hammerstein and George Gershwin. The area shifted to a predominantly African American demographic in the 1920s and 1930s, during the Harlem Renaissance. Part of the area was known as "Sugar Hill," because wealthy African Americans enjoyed the "sweet" life in the area. Residents included W.E.B. Du Bois, Thurgood Marshall, Adam Clayton Powell and Duke Ellington.

Now, the area's demographics have shifted once again. There is a Hispanic majority, many of whom are Dominican, a sizable African American population and some West Indians and whites. For the most part, the neighborhood has steered clear of gentrification. The area is culturally and ethnically diverse.

People in the neighborhood vary in their age range. There are many families with young children, yet there are also students, young professionals and an older population. The residents are very friendly, and there is a strong sense of community. Young men sit on the sidewalk braiding their hair or playing dominoes. Teenagers hang out in groups on the sidewalks, talking until late at night. When it is sweltering outside, locals break open the fire hydrants for car washes or for kids to play in. The neighborhood's parks are crowded at all times of day, whether it is with older, homeless men talking, young men playing basketball or kids playing.

Hamilton Heights is home to City College of New York (CCNY), City University's oldest institution and flagship campus. The campus has several breath-taking, neo-Gothic buildings, mixed in with a few buildings that have a more modern flare.

St. Nicholas Park runs along the eastern border of City College. The hilly, tree-filled park has basketball courts, playgrounds and barbecue areas. Large families and groups of friends make use of the barbecue areas, creating a wholesome family activity and delicious-smelling feasts.

Restaurants and Bars

Most of the restaurants and retail stores in Hamilton Heights are located either on Broadway Avenue or 145th Street. Fast food is anything but sparse in Hamilton Heights, whether you are looking for McDonald's, Burger King or Dunkin Donuts. In addition to fast food, the area has countless delis and small grocery stores, offering many options for inexpensive food. There are also a handful of small restaurants, where you can easily pick up inexpensive Mexican or Chinese cuisine. Street vendors sell fresh fruit, ice cream, corn or other treats to the area's residents. There is a great variety of food options in Hamilton Heights, many with a foreign flavor. Unfortunately, it is lacking in nice, sit-down restaurants.

While there are not many bars in the area, many of the streets remain vibrant and active at night. Some of the delis and restaurants stay open all night, providing plenty to do for those who stay up late. However, this could be a negative aspect for those seeking a quiet respite from the downtown noise.

Parks and Recreation

Riverside Park, a quaint beautiful path that runs along the west side of Hamilton Heights, is usually populated by people walking their dogs or relaxing on a bench. For those looking for more excitement, Riverbank State Park is accessible by bridge from Riverside Park. The 28-acre park has everything -- a swimming pool, skating rink, cultural theater, athletic complex with a fitness room, basketball courts, tennis courts, restaurant and a carousel. The park is open long hours and full of activity, including young kids at camp, adults working out and families using the pool. The park also offers beautiful views of the Hudson River and New Jersey.

Transportation

It is easy to get from Hamilton Heights to other areas of Manhattan. The 1, A, B, C and D trains all stop in Hamilton Heights, and the trip takes only 20 minutes to Times Square and 45 minutes to lower Manhattan. For those who can't find enough excitement in Hamilton Heights, it is a quick trip downtown for bars and nice restaurants.

Harlem

Jordan Rubenstein is a human rights advocate and freelance writer. She currently works at Congregation Beit Simchat Torah, the world's largest lesbian, gay, bisexual, and transgender (LGBT) synagogue. As a writer for Change.org and Next Magazine, she spends much of her free time advocating for human rights. Jordan eagerly moved to New York City after graduating from Carnegie Mellon University in Pittsburgh.

The Good News

1. Culture.
In the 1920s and 1930s, Harlem was home to the Harlem Renaissance, a culture movement with great emphasis on the arts. Harlem continues to celebrate the arts and is also the center of African American culture. The neighborhood has a unique and strong emphasis on culture and community.

2. Lots to do.
Want to go shopping? 125th Street has many stores, including major clothing store chains. Interested in playing sports outdoors? Harlem has parks with swimming pools, recreation centers, baseball fields, and more. Or, if you prefer a nice night out, Harlem has many restaurants to choose from, a movie theater, and performances at the Apollo Theater.

3. Variety.
The different areas of Harlem have entirely different feels. Someone interested in lots of activity would enjoy living near 125th Street, while someone interested in a quiet respite from the rest of Manhattan would enjoy living a little further north. The neighborhood is uniquely varied and has something for everyone.

The Bad News

1. Poverty and Crime.

The area has higher rates of poverty and crime than other parts of town and unemployment rates are far higher than the New York average. But crime has plummeted significantly in the last 20 years, and Harlem is much safer than you may expect.

2. Reputation.

Sure, Harlem is safer than it used to be, but not everyone got the memo. Tell your friends that you live in Harlem, and they may avoid visiting you. Many people think of poverty and crime when they think of Harlem. Few people realize all great things Harlem has to offer.

3. Gentrification.

Retail developments on 125th Street and new housing developments led to huge increases in property values in the 1990s. Gentrification has ultimately made the neighborhood unaffordable for some people and forced them into surrounding neighborhoods. However, Harlem is still affordable compared to many other areas of New York City.

Harlem

Harlem has quite a reputation, both in New York City and across the country. Some think of it as a crime-laden area where poor people live. Others recognize it as a neighborhood with a strong culture and an interesting history. This large neighborhood has streets lined with retail stores and restaurants, quiet streets with beautiful rows of brownstones and everything in between.

Central Harlem spans from the top of Central Park at 110th Street all the way to 155th Street. While Harlem technically encompasses the area from The Hudson River on the west to the Harlem River on the right, Central Harlem spans the width of Central Park.

Demographics

Due to the size and variation within Harlem, it appeals to a wide range of residents. The area is home to people of all age ranges. Students from nearby colleges (Harlem borders City College and Columbia University), young professionals, families and elderly people all live in Harlem. The area near Columbia University and 125th Street is particularly appealing for those who like vibrant nightlife and activity, while those seeking a quiet, quaint home may want to check out the more northern areas of Harlem.

Parks and Recreation

There are several very nice parks within the boundaries of Central Harlem. Marcus Garvey Park (better known as Mount Morris Park) has a recreation center, amphitheater, swimming pool, playgrounds, baseball field and a dog run. Jackie Robinson Park runs from 145th Street (right across the street from one of Harlem's three Starbucks locations) all the way up to 155th Street. The narrow park has a swimming pool, a recreation center, baseball fields, basketball courts, volleyball courts and playgrounds.

History

True appreciation of Harlem culture comes from an understanding of the neighborhood's history. In the 1920s and 1930s, the Harlem Renaissance (which, at the time, was known as the "New Negro Movement") became a powerful cultural movement in Harlem. During this period, New York City had a growing African American middle class demographic. Harlem, in particular, was largely African American starting in the early 1900s. During the Harlem Renaissance, great emphasis was placed on the arts, such as writing, theater and music. Specifically, jazz music was popular, and Harlem was home to jazz nightclubs where musicians performed.

The most well-known physical legacy of the Harlem Renaissance is the Apollo Theater, which opened in 1914. Located on 125th Street, it is a symbol for African American culture. Billie Holiday, Ella Fitzgerald, Sarah Vaughan and many others started their careers at the Apollo. While the theater had a decline in business in the late 1960s, it now draws 1.3 million visitors each year.

The Apollo wasn't the only business in Harlem that struggled in the 1960s. During the Great Depression and the deindustrialization in New York following World War II, crime and poverty grew in Harlem. As New York City was economically revived in the late 1900s, Harlem improved economically as well, leading to gentrification in the area. During this period of gentrification, city policies focused on crime prevention and retail development on 125th Street. New housing developments were also funded, and property values in Central Harlem increased by almost 300 percent in the 1990s. Several huge housing projects that were developed by the 1960s allow less affluent residents to live in Harlem despite rising property values.

Both in the Harlem Renaissance and today, Harlem is a center of African American culture. A significant part of the neighborhood, including a majority of businesses in Harlem, is owned by African Americans.

In 1950, Harlem was 98.2 percent African American. Not long after, many middle class African Americans moved to the outer boroughs. Now, there are growing numbers of Hispanic and white residents, yet the area still has a black majority. The annual African American Day Parade takes place in Harlem as a celebration of African American culture.

Restaurants, Shopping, and Churches

Nowadays, 125th Street continues to flourish. The streets are crowded with street vendors and area residents. 125th Street is the place to go for shopping -- one can find Old Navy, H&M, Modells, Gamestop and CVS. There is also a huge movie theater and Bill Clinton's office (which has been located at 55 West 125th Street since 2001).

Central Harlem has a wide variety of restaurants. The area has chains such as Applebee's and IHOP and fast food options ranging from McDonalds to Quiznos. The neighborhood also has many smaller, local restaurants. There are many soul food restaurants to choose from as well as other options, including Italian, Mexican, and Mediterranean.

Harlem is a religious area, dominated by several Christian denominations, including Baptists, Methodists, Episcopalians and Roman Catholics. There are over 400 churches in Harlem, as well as several mosques, a Mormon church and a few synagogues. Many of the more beautiful buildings in Harlem are huge, impressive churches.

Poverty and Crime

The area struggles with disproportionate rates of poverty and crime. Unemployment rates are approximately twice as high as the New York average. In the 1940s, there were about 100 murders per year in Harlem; the majority of drug addicts in New York City lived in Harlem; and juvenile delinquency was far higher in Harlem than the rest of New York City. Because drug use was popular in Harlem, crimes, such as stealing and violence, increased. Recently, crime has significantly plummeted. In the last 20 years, crimes including murder, rape, robbery and burglary have all dropped substantially. Harlem has kept its poor reputation in regards to crime, but the area is generally safe.

With its reputation for poverty and crime, many people will make the mistake of avoiding Harlem. But for those with an open mind, Harlem truly has something for everyone.

Washington Heights

Sarah Badger is a native Texan and recent graduate of Marymount Manhattan College where she studied English and Religions. Her writing has appeared in literary journals, Dance Spirit magazine, and The Sigma Tau Delta Rectangle for which she won the Elizabeth Holtze award in creative nonfiction. A classically-trained dancer, Sarah recently danced with In-Sight Dance Company in Queens and has performed in theme parks, industrials, and various showcases throughout New York City. Sarah lived in Northern Manhattan for several years before relocating to Houghton, NY with her husband Graham.

The Good News:

1. Affordability
Washington Heights is widely recognized as the most affordable area of Manhattan. You'll pay less than your neighbors in Harlem and the Upper West Side and still be just a subway ride away from midtown Manhattan.

2. Community
Washington Heights has long been home to immigrant communities. Today, Dominican-Americans dominate these Northern Manhattan blocks, bringing with them a strong sense of community and emphasis on family life. Area parks and recreational centers allow neighbors to congregate for weekend picnics, barbecues, and soccer games.

3. Accessibility
Serviced by the A, 1, C trains, and the George Washington Bus Depot, Washington Heights residents can get to New Jersey, the Bronx, and many Manhattan neighborhoods in less than a half-hour. Commutes to Brooklyn and Queens may prove more lengthy, but those who work in Manhattan will enjoy the convenience of Washington Heights living.

The Bad News:

1. Language Barriers

If you don't speak Spanish, you may find it difficult to communicate with some of your neighbors. Cultural life in Washington Heights might make you feel more like you're living in the Dominican Republic than New York City. While people in "the Heights" tend to be welcoming and friendly, newcomers may feel culturally isolated for a while.

2. It's No Beauty

Although Washington Heights is a lively, vibrant neighborhood, it's not the most picturesque. A high population density and run-down buildings give the area classically unkempt, urban feel. With some exceptions, neighborhood bars and restaurants tend to feel as grimy as their surroundings.

3. Limited Dining

If you're a fan of Dominican and Caribbean-inspired cuisine, Washington Heights has plenty to offer, though it lacks culinary diversity. Beyond a few pizzerias and Chinese restaurants, the Heights has little to offer aside from Latin American food, so diners in the neighborhood may quickly become bored.

Washington Heights

Stretching North from Harlem to the very tip of the island of Manhattan, Washington Heights and Inwood remain among the most diverse cultural communities in Manhattan, New York. Washington Heights, sometimes called "WaHi" or, simply, "The Heights," encompasses the fifty blocks just north of Harlem from West 155th to Dyckman Street. Inwood encompasses the remaining northern blocks of the island. The Harlem River separates Inwood from Marble Hill and the Bronx. While Washington Heights and Inwood maintain distinct characteristics, their similarities and geographic proximity have resulted in many economic and demographic overlaps.

History and Demographics

Washington Heights earned its name from Fort Washington, an important military base constructed during the American Revolution. Today, a plaque commemorates the former site of Fort Washington in Bennett Park near West 183rd Street. The site also marks the highest natural point in Manhattan, where Bennett Park now stands at 263 feet above sea level. Because of its altitude relative to most of Manhattan, many Washington Heights streets are steep and hilly. Some residents use the elevators inside of the area's subway stations to simplify the travel between higher and lower blocks in the neighborhood.

Development continued in Washington Heights following the American Revolution, with a great number of Irish and German immigrants inhabiting the neighborhood throughout the 19th century. A wave of Jewish immigrants settled in Washington Heights following Hitler's rise to power in the 1930s, while a Greek community began to flourish in the neighborhood in the 1950s. Later in the twentieth century, communities of Puerto Rican, Dominican and other Latin Americans began calling The Heights home.

Meanwhile, Washington Height's immigrant communities also found homes in Inwood; the area maintained a distinctly Irish identity well into the twentieth century. Remnants of Inwood's Irish community now inhabit the western blocks of the neighborhood close to the Hudson River. While Washington Heights saw commercial development throughout its history, Inwood remained largely residential. A few stone quarries brought economic growth to Inwood in its early years of development but quickly moved south. As a result, the neighborhood feels much more suburban than most of Washington Heights.

Today, both neighborhoods are predominately Dominican, with lower income families dominating the eastern half of the neighborhood and more affluent residents claiming the buildings and townhouses on the west side. Both neighborhoods contain several "sub-neighborhoods" with distinct names and characteristics. Locals sometimes refer to the area east of Broadway near 190th Street "Fort George" and the eastern border of Inwood "Sherman Creek" due to its proximity to the body of water of the same name. The blocks west of Broadway are known alternately as "Hudson Heights" or "Fort Tryon."

Parks and Recreation

A typical Northern Manhattan family might begin their day with the children walking to one of the several public or private schools throughout Northern Manhattan. Working adults in the household would likely take the bus or subway to work. Bodegas, delis, convenience stores and restaurants provide some jobs in the neighborhood, but the vast majority of Inwood and Washington Heights residents work in more commercial Manhattan neighborhoods. The Metropolitan Transit Authority services Northern Manhattan on the A, C and 1 train lines. The Metro-North railway station in Inwood allows residents easy access to Westchester and Connecticut, while easy transportation to New Jersey is available via the George Washington Bus Terminal in Washington Heights.

Schools, religious institutions, and parks line the streets of Washington Heights and Inwood. Fort Tryon Park, home of the Cloister's branch of the Metropolitan Museum of Art, attracts many visitors to Northern Manhattan. Located in a sub-neighborhood called Hudson Heights, the park overlooks the Hudson River and New Jersey's Palisades. Highbridge Park runs along the Harlem River on the eastern side of the neighborhood. Unlike Fort Tryon, Highbridge Park is home to many recreational sports facilities including basketball courts, baseball diamonds and swimming pools. Inwood boasts the last remaining natural forest in Manhattan at Inwood Hill Park. In addition to the rugged hiking paths, trees and views of the Harlem and Hudson rivers, Inwood Hill Park contains tennis courts, fields, ponds, and playgrounds popular with neighborhood children.

Weekends in Washington Heights and Inwood often include youth soccer games in Highbridge and Inwood Hill Park and block parties. The area's immigrant roots contribute to the strong sense of community found throughout the area, and it is not uncommon for neighbors to enjoy picnics and games and music together on apartment stoops.

Housing

Although some upper-middle class owners occupy condos, co-ops and townhouses, rentals dominate the Upper Manhattan real estate market. Most of the area's residential structures are prewar buildings between five and ten stories tall. Most residents belong to working class families, though some students and artists come to Northern Manhattan to take advantage of low rents and larger apartments. The majority of the neighborhood's post-secondary students attend Columbia University's medical school on West 168th Street or Yeshiva University in Fort George.

Apart from claiming some of the lowest rents in Manhattan, residents of Northern Manhattan enjoy quick access to Midtown, New Jersey, and surrounding suburbs as well as some of the most scenic views in the city. The abundance of trees and botany in Inwood make the area smell fresher than other more isolated parts of the city. Those who appreciate strong community identities tend to like the atmosphere in Northern Manhattan, where neighbors often take the time to get to know one another.

Of course, life in Washington Heights or Inwood is not for everyone. Residents, who don't speak Spanish, might find it difficult to communicate with some neighbors or feel culturally isolated. While a few nightclubs have moved into the area recently, there are few options for extroverts who seek exciting night life. Many bars and restaurants have a dingy, unkempt feel. Dominican and Latin restaurants dominate the culinary landscape of Northern Manhattan, but other choices are somewhat limited. Diners with special dietary needs may find it difficult to dine out in Washington Heights and Inwood. Additionally, commuting to neighborhoods on the east side of Manhattan or in other boroughs (besides the Bronx) can be tiresome and lengthy. Even with these drawbacks, Washington Heights and Inwood continue to grow and evolve, opening their arms to new residents looking for a corner of Manhattan to call home.

Hudson Heights (Fort Tryon)

Sarah Badger is a native Texan and recent graduate of Marymount Manhattan College where she studied English and Religions. Her writing has appeared in literary journals, Dance Spirit magazine, and The Sigma Tau Delta Rectangle for which she won the Elizabeth Holtze award in creative nonfiction. A classically-trained dancer, Sarah recently danced with In-Sight Dance Company in Queens and has performed in theme parks, industrials, and various showcases throughout New York City. Sarah lived in Northern Manhattan for several years before relocating to Houghton, NY with her husband Graham.

The Good News

1. *Affordability.*
Hudson Heights residents don't have to leave Manhattan to live affordably in New York City. Many rentals run you even less per month than equally sized units in the outer boroughs. With a slightly heavier wallet, you can enjoy those breathtaking views of the Hudson River even more.

2. *Beauty.*
Astounding art-deco architecture, pristine parks, and preserved natural landscapes set this Western enclave apart from neighboring Washington Heights. The sloping streets, quiet atmosphere, and accessibility to the medieval Cloisters Museum in Fort Tryon make the neighborhood feel like an escape from the hustle, bustle, and grime of the city, while still rendering all the benefits of a Manhattan zip-code.

3. *Community.*
If you're a fan of families and getting to know your neighbors, you'll love Hudson Heights living. Rising rents in other traditionally family-friendly areas of New York City have contributed to the growing number of families with children residing in the area.   Those who live in this neighborhood make an effort to look out for each other and encourage community activities and involvement.

The Bad News

1. *Long commutes.*

Heed Duke Ellington's advice to "take the A train", but skip the Harlem stops and climb all the way up to the sloping streets of Hudson Heights. While express service on the A train takes uptown commuters to midtown in just 20 minutes, if you need to get downtown or to the East side you're in for a long ride. Commuters in need of daytime local service will need to walk to nearest 1 train in Washington Heights or make a transfer.

2. *Limited entertainment.*

This is not the action-packed New York of Hollywood movies. Although the Cloisters museum is nearby, and you can easily walk across Broadway for a few theaters and music venues, entertainment options are limited. Those in search of nightlife will need to hop on a subway or bus, or hail a cab to experience the Manhattan club scene.

3. *Dining options.*

A handful of sit-down restaurants make their home in Hudson Heights, along with a few delis and take-out joints. Although the dining options in the area continue to expand, it's far from a culinary oasis.

Life in Hudson Heights

The Hudson Heights neighborhood in the heart of Upper Manhattan has adopted almost as many different names as it has kinds of residents. Alternately known as "Fort Tryon," the hilly neighborhood borders Washington Heights on the east and the Hudson River on the west. Fort Tryon Park provides the northern boundary, and the George Washington Bridge at 180th Street provides a rough southern border. George Washington first used the area now known as Hudson Heights as the sight of Fort Washington, an important military base during the American Revolution. During the early twentieth century, the area became home to an influx of immigrants, largely from Ireland and Germany. The German immigrant population grew so much before and after World War II that New Yorkers began calling the area "Frankfurt-on-the-Hudson." Today, various immigrant and ethnic communities continue to call Hudson Heights home, while the low cost of living and quiet atmosphere attract retired individuals, young families and students.

Demographics and Housing

The growing differences between the demographics of Hudson Heights and the surrounding Washington Heights have helped solidify the former as a distinct sub-community worthy of special consideration. A Latino population--

mostly of Dominican descent--dominates buildings further east and many of the rentals throughout Hudson Heights. The neighborhood's proximity to Yeshiva University and its German-Jewish immigrant past have made it home to a prominent Jewish Orthodox community, particularly along Bennett and Fort Washington Avenues. While rentals represent a significant portion of Hudson Heights' real estate, condos and co-ops dominate the westernmost residential streets. The upper-middle class families live in purchased one and two bedroom apartments overlooking the Hudson River along Cabrini Boulevard and Pinehurst Avenue. Medical students at the nearby Columbia-Presbyterian Hospital, along with undergraduate and graduate students from Yeshiva University and other colleges throughout the city, occupy a portion of the rented apartments. Lower-income families and single working professionals make up the remainder of the rental community, making Hudson Heights one of the most socio-economically diverse areas in Manhattan.

Yeshiva University and Columbia-Presbyterian Hospital students and staff enjoy a quick walk to work or school, while most other Hudson Heights residents take the express A train from the 190th or 181st Street stations to work in midtown, downtown or the Upper West Side. The M4 bus also provides service from Hudson Heights to the Upper East Side and Penn Station.

Parks and Recreation

A Hudson Heights resident might begin the day by walking
their dog through Bennett Park, Manhattan's highest natural
point.   The neighborhood's many parks and playgrounds
attract pet owners, as well as parents with small children.
On weekends, parents accompany their kids to Fort Tryon's
large, renovated playground on the northern end of the
park, while art connoisseurs in the area might pay a visit to
the Cloisters Museum. John D. Rockefeller commissioned
the construction of the museum in the 1930s, and it houses
much of the Metropolitan Museum of Art's medieval
collection. Completed in 1938 and built stone-by-stone from
the remains of real medieval cloisters and castles imported
from Europe, the Cloisters Museum overlooks New Jersey's
Palisades Park, directly across the river from Hudson
Heights. The serenity and lack of urban-development attract
many New Yorkers who desire a respite from city life
without having to leave Manhattan.

Restaurants and Retail

After a busy day exploring the park, families and singles
alike might relax and enjoy a meal at one of the restaurants
along 181st and 187th Streets. Unlike other areas of
Washington Heights where Latin cooking reigns supreme,
no one variety of cuisine dominates the blocks west of
Broadway. Thai curries, tacos, and sushi rolls are all available

alongside traditional New York-style diners and plenty of hole-in-the-wall Chinese takeout joints. Some establishments with adjoining bars and lounges offer live music on weekends, but generally diners will need to look outside of the neighborhood for post-dinner entertainment and nightlife.

Because the neighborhood is known for its suburban-like quality relative to the rest of Manhattan, the majority of Hudson Heights' residents tend to prefer evenings at home, rather than nights on the town. Residents who enjoy nightlife may become frustrated with constant subway trips to favorite nightspots downtown, particularly with the lack of express subway service during late nights and weekends. Other potential inconveniences accompany a Hudson Heights life as well. Even with the variety of new dining establishments opening their doors along the commercial hubs of Fort Washington Avenue and 181st Street, the area lacks the array of culinary choices usually characteristic of Manhattan life. Additionally, indoor entertainment options are limited mostly to the Cloisters Museum and a tiny run-down movie theater just west of Broadway on 181st Street. Bibliophiles will have to hop on the train or bus to find a bookstore, or walk to the nearest libraries in Washington Heights and Inwood. Although mom-and-pop stores, bodegas and markets still meet the shopping needs of many Hudson Heights residents, fast food restaurants, a Starbucks, and a mid-size supermarket chain have filled empty storefronts in recent years (to the delight of some and the

chagrin of others). Hudson Heights' location on the northern
tip of the island also makes some daily commutes lengthy
and troublesome. While the A train provides speedy service
along Manhattan's west side, residents, who work further
downtown on the east side or in other boroughs, will find
themselves spending as many as two hours in transit daily.
Despite these drawbacks, Hudson Heights continues to
attract newcomers seeking an ever-changing community to
call home.

Little Italy / Nolita

JM Tohline is a novelist and freelance writer whose love of "those little pockets inside each city that tourists never see" has carried him from Coast to Coast and everywhere in between. Someday, he will own a pet fox and name it Kerouac.

The Good News

1. *History.*

Little Italy is one of the most history-rich areas of Manhattan, and between the cobbled streets and the overabundance of red, green, and white, you are sure to get a vibrant dose of this history every day.

2. *Daily Feast.*

From Lombardi's Pizzeria on Spring Street to the cafés of Mulberry Street to Parisi Bakery and Di Palo's Fine Foods, there is no shortage of rapturous, Old World eatin' in Little Italy.

3. *Annual Feast.*

The annual Feast of San Gennaro, originally a one-day tribute to the patron saint of Naples, has now become an 11-day smorgasbord of food, drink, and very little sleep.

The Bad News

1. *"Littler" Italy.*
Little Italy has become progressively squeezed out by the ever-expanding edge of Chinatown, so while the history remains, the anchors that hold that history in place are rapidly losing their grip on the ground.

2. *Nolita - No Longer Italy.*
Nolita (NOrth of Little ITAly) has become an upscale neighborhood overflowing with expensive boutiques and trendy restaurants and bars, losing the once-distinctive "Little Italy" flavor. While Nolita offers the thinned-out streets of an upscale, non-tourist area, the Italian flavor has mostly evaporated.

3. *Know Your Neighbor? Not so much.*
Little Italy is endlessly crowded with tourists passing through for the day, and very little of the once-distinctive "small community" Little Italy aura still exists today.

Little Italy / Nolita

The narrow, cobbled streets beneath your feet; the overabundance of red, green and white; the rapturous aroma of Italian food; and the thick, Italian accents that you assumed only existed in movies—these were once the trademarks of Little Italy in Lower Manhattan.

If you visited Little Italy thirty years ago, you experienced a transformation from the rest of the city. In fact, you experienced what felt like a transportation to another part of the world. Little Italy grew from the immigration boom of the 1800s, and, as thousands of Italians settled into this pocket of the city, they carried with them their Old World allegiances. Each group of Italians carved out their own little piece of the city. While the Western Sicilians settled down on Elizabeth Street, the Northern Italians landed on Bleecker Street, and the Genoese made their home on Baxter Street. These segregated groups of Italians combined to create an ambiance that reminded them of home, which still attracts scores of tourists to the area today.

Of course, the "today" of Little Italy is much different from what you might have found not too long ago. While nearly 70,000 Italians moved to this part of the city between 1860 and 1880, only a few thousand remain in the neighborhood today. As Little Italy has become "Littler Italy," it has lost some of its former magic; however, there is still plenty to appreciate for visitors and residents alike.

The biggest draw for visitors is the annual Feast of San Gennaro. What began in 1926 as a one-day tribute to the patron saint of Naples (and, rather ironically, as a means by which to provide charity to those in need) has ballooned into an 11-day extravaganza celebrating Italian culture. More than one million people visit Little Italy between the second Thursday of September and the end of the festival, enjoying everything from music to parades to—what else!—a cannoli-eating contest.

Dining

Throughout the rest of the year, residents gather to catch both a lingering taste of the Italian ambiance that once ran so thick in the neighborhood and a fresh taste of the Italian food that is ubiquitous even now. Lombardi's Pizzeria on Spring Street is considered to be the oldest pizzeria in the United States, and Parisi Bakery and Di Palo's Fine Foods offer classic, historic Italian experiences. Mulberry Street is also full of cafes that provide ample street-sitting, people-watching opportunities. Along this street you are likely to not only be tempted by the smells of the restaurants, but also by the waiters, who are often found calling to passersby in an effort to lure them inside. Although many of these eateries have been in place for ages, most of their business now comes from once-and-done tourists. While the heyday of Little

Italy would have given you an authentic, residential eating experience, you would now be as likely to run into a Californian in one of the restaurants as you would an Italian.

Change

The primary cause for the shrinkage of Little Italy has been the expansion of next-door neighbor Chinatown, but, even before the edges of Little Italy began to bleed away, it was breaking apart from the inside. While the boundaries of Little Italy once stretched north of Kenmare, all the way up to Bleecker, the exit of many Italian-Americans from the area caused an entire section of Little Italy to lose its Italian flavor. The area between Houston and Broome (north and south), and Bowery and Lafeyette (east and west) saw a sudden shift during the 1990s into an upscale neighborhood overflowing with expensive boutiques and trendy restaurants and bars. This area became known as Nolita ("NOrth of Little ITAly"), and it has quickly taken on a personality altogether different from the history from which it grew.

Housing

In both Little Italy and Nolita, the majority of residents live in the six-story, turn-of-the-century tenements that once housed Italian families and all their Old World traditions. Condominiums are also common in the area. Although, these are more likely to be found in Nolita than in Little Italy, as the sudden swing toward upscale living in Nolita has influenced alterations in the available residential options. While the upward jump in lifestyle has made Nolita among the more expensive living choices in Manhattan, it has also thinned out the traffic. Little Italy, on the other hand, is crowded with the sort of persistence that can make a local's throat tighten, especially when considering that the crowds are mostly tourists passing through for the day.

Transportation

As for leaving Little Italy and Nolita, both areas are central pieces of the Metropolitan Transportation Authority (MTA). From all points of these neighborhoods you can hop on a subway and—without switching lines—reach Brooklyn, Queens, the Bronx and Upper Manhattan, and several bus routes run right through the area.

Conclusion

While there are certainly drawbacks to the lifestyle of what once was Little Italy—the flock of tourists on Mulberry; the pricey living in Nolita; the ebb of true Italian flavor—the streets are still rich with history, and the area is full of New York City magic. It might not be the authentic Italian experience it was in the past, but the area that once was Little Italy is a gem of culture and history all the same.

Greenpoint

Perrin Drumm is a California-born, Brooklyn-based writer with strong feelings about design, architecture, art and film. She is currently working on her MFA in Fiction. You can see her work at flavors.me/perrindrumm.

The Good News

1. Eating Out.
With it's mix of cheap, old world staples and bevy of new bars that include good ol' hangs, craft beer havens (Brouwerjii Lane, Pencil Factory) and serious card-carrying mixologists (Manhattan Inn) and restaurants serving up lovingly baked brick oven pizza (Paulie Gee's) as well as places nice enough to impress your folks when they're in town (Anella, 5 Leaves), you'll never go hungry or thirsty in Greenpoint.

2. Shopping.
Greenpoint has become something of a shopping destination in recent years, with new boutiques cropping up on Franklin Street each month, literally. Original, much-loved standbys like WORD bookstore and B's Bikes are now in good company with music shops (Permanent Records, Pentatonic Guitars), men's and women's clothing (Alter, In God We Trust, Dalaga, Hayden Harnett) and vintage and antique stores (Old Hollywood, Le Grenier, Kill Devil Hill) that even Manhattanites stop over to check out.

3. Location.
Being the northernmost point of Brooklyn means easy access to Long Island City and Queens, a straight shot South into the rest of Brooklyn and, as it's situated right on the East River, a relatively painless hop West into the city.

The Bad News

1. The G Train

Even though Greenpoint does have certain geographical advantages, the G train is not one of them. The unreliable, often late or completely absent subway line is the bane of every Greenpointer's existence. Luckily, the buses stick to a schedule, the L isn't too far away and let us not forget every Brooklynites best friend, the bike.

2. Diversity

If you're looking for a multi-cultural experience, Greenpoint is not for you. The neighborhood is basically divided in half, between the younger American newcomers and the older Polish-speaking, Polish-eating and Polish-drinking generation

3. Post-Industrial Waste

Though most of Greenpoint's abandoned, turn-of-the-century warehouses have been repurposed as housing or other commercial spaces, there are still a few reminders of the days of yore, namely the notoriously polluted Newtown Creek and the drug-infested Greenpoint Hotel, both of which are easily avoided and are currently undergoing major rehabilitation.

Greenpoint

Before it was a turn-of-the-century industrial port town, before the British set up camp there during the Revolutionary War and before the first Dutch immigrants staked it out for farmland, Greenpoint, like much of Manhattan, was a lush, open space originally settled by the Keskachauge Indian tribe. Separated from Long Island City (LIC) by Newtown Creek to the north, flanked by the East River and nestled just above Williamsburg, Greenpoint is Brooklyn's northernmost neighborhood and the closest to Manhattan. Its proximity to the big island made it ideal farmland for the Dutch, who took their produce to Manhattan by boat. The streets of Greenpoint (which run alphabetical from north to south) pay homage to the farmers Calyer and Meserole, who were the very first to build homes and cultivate the land.

The Past

At the peak of the Industrial Revolution, when Greenpoint was at the forefront of shipbuilding and maritime commerce, a new immigrant group took over, and the neighborhood was dubbed "Little Poland" from then on. Most of these waterfront warehouses are still around, as are many original Polish businesses, mostly butcher shops and bakeries, that dot Manhattan Avenue, the primary commercial street.

The neighborhood still relied on industry in 1950, when the largest United States oil spill at the time flooded Newtown Creek. An estimated 17 to 30 million gallons of oil spilled out and has been leaking into the groundwater ever since. The results of government studies of the area under the EPA (Environmental Protection Agency) are vague, and, given the fact that in the last 60 years only half of the damage has been cleaned up, many residents are still suspicious of harmful side effects, though no concrete evidence has been found.

Change

Industry prevailed into the 1980s, and Greenpoint was a typical, working class neighborhood. Streets were lined with brick row houses, and Manhattan Avenue boasted a movie theatre and skating rink. But, when the gentrification that took root in Williamsburg traveled north, rents spiked, leaving many families displaced. Still, Poles have an overwhelming presence in Greenpoint today. Many families date back more than three generations, making Greenpoint the second highest Polish concentration in the U.S., third only to Poland itself. However, that may be about to change. With the 2005 zoning laws and the fleet of shiny, new condo buildings that have sprung up along the water, gentrification is in full force. Nearly 20,000 new residents are expected to move in by next year, something the Polish population isn't too happy about.

Out and About

Walk down any street in Greenpoint and the divide between the old world Polish feel and the influx of young artists in their twenties and thirties is obvious. By day, Polish grandmothers do their marketing in long skirts and patterned head kerchiefs, and Polish-speaking restaurants like Karczma serve pierogis, kielbasa, hunter's stew and stuffed cabbage all for under $10, topped off with a side order of peasant-style lard. Many of the Polish-owned bars have "Members Only" signs on their doors, and their lackluster interiors and windows crowded with neon beer signs stick out against the latest crop of more design-forward bars serving up well-groomed cocktail menus aimed to attract the 'gentrification generation.' Greenpoint is also the home of the now famous Rooftop Farms on Eagle Street, which provides organic, sustainably grown produce to local restaurants. It's just off Franklin Street, where new boutiques and cafes pop up every month, making it one of the boroughs best shopping destinations.

The disparity between old and new is one of the charms of the neighborhood, and it's why so many new residents and families are flocking to the area. Of course, it has its downside. While Greenpoint may be just across the water from Manhattan, it's connected by the G train, notorious for its long waits and erratic schedule. Luckily, the vastly more reliable L train is only a connection away, and those on bike can make the short ride south and take the newly revamped Williamsburg Bridge into the city or head north into LIC for the 7 train. And, as Brooklyn itself is the most bike-friendly borough, you can be in Bushwick, Williamsburg or LIC in well under 10 minutes.

Housing

One of Greenpoint's major attractions for renters and buyers is its proximity to the hubbub of new waterfront condos that surround Kent Street's East River Park. While the park is quickly becoming the center of social activity in the area (it hosts an impressive lineup of bands every weekend, with even more public outdoor spaces that run the length of the water well under way), preserving Greenpoint's distinctive feel means keeping those brand new condos south of the border. So far, only a few new developers have crept into Greenpoint, and residents aren't in favor of 20-story condos sitting side-by-side with historic four-floor walk-ups. Still, a change is clearly underway. While the century-old industrial warehouses that speckle the Brooklyn skyline are an ever present reminder of a century gone by, those memories are learning to share space with the new developments that are making Greenpoint some of the most sought after real estate in Brooklyn.

East Village

by Lindsey Sikes

The East Village

Once you've gotten past the fast-paced overload of glitz, glam, skyscrapers and get-out-of-my-way-or-get-run-down taxi drivers that draw so many to the Big Apple, you'll be pleasantly surprised to find that in this big city there exists a place where you can have it all and still feel like you're home. Named appropriately, both for the location on the lower east side of Manhattan and for the temperament of the area, the East Village is the kind of place where you feel like part of a community. The Village, as it is more commonly referred to, offers just about everything you're looking for, but on a less intimidating scale. Ready to put on the pumps and head out for a night of debauchery? There are plenty of local bars, clubs and venues where you'll find excitement. Or would you rather to take it easy and soak up the local culture for an afternoon? Then all you have to do is walk around the corner to your local deli, grab a sandwich and head a few blocks to the nearest park, where you won't be the only one lounging in the grass on a sunny New York day.

The East Village encompasses the area of Manhattan from 5th Avenue to the East River, above Houston street and below 14th street (give or take a few blocks depending on who you talk to). The feel and locale of the Village changes quite a bit, though, as you head from East to West.

At the west-most end you'll find Washington Square Park and the center of the New York University campus. Besides being considered the best place to feed the massive NYC squirrels or kick up your heels in the giant fountain, the park is most famous for its architecture—specifically, the arch. According to legend, locals used to be able to enter the arch and climb the stairs to the hollowed-out top, until one night a group of young adults became so inebriated that they refused to leave—threatening dissent and anarchy through their wine-soaked teeth. Since then, the doors have been sealed, but the arch remains a valuable historical landmark in the area. However, WSP isn't always a great escape. You will usually find a large majority of college students inhabiting this area of the village. The overcrowding of NYU students has caused many complaints from long-time residents of the Village, but if you're immune to 20-something hipsters you may not even notice the heavily saturated student population.

Further east leads you to 3rd, 2nd and 1st avenues, where you'll find great local eateries, street shopping, tattoo parlors and plenty of bars. St. Marks Street, located a block east of Astor Place between 3rd and 2nd Avenues, is infamous for the array of tattoo parlors, specialty shops and food spots cheaper than you can find anywhere else in the city. One such place is 2 Bros. Pizza, with $1 New York sized pizza slices sure to leave you smiling.

Beyond 1st Avenue you enter Alphabet City, so named because the avenues begin to go by letters rather than numbers. Much of Alphabet City is a nice, family-friendly place where there's a deli on every corner, plenty of small parks and historic tenement buildings which are now rented by a majority of young adults. As you stroll through the neighborhood, you'll find lots filled with community art, buildings of every color imaginable, and just about any type of cuisine you could be craving—from Indian to Sushi to Mexican. However, the further east you go, the more dangerous these neighborhoods do become. Beyond Avenue D, closer to the East River, there is a significant increase in gang and criminal activity.

Though the feel of the east village changes as you move from one end to the next, there is a distinct quality about the people who call themselves "Villagers"—from moms and dads pushing strollers to hipsters in their latest vintage thrift finds. There is a certain je ne sais quoi about the Village that can best be described as "boho-trendy". And while the large population of villagers are students or young professionals without an artistic bone in their body, most like to think they are hipper than the average, well...average joe.

But that's not to say that everyone you'll encounter is a "poser" in some way. In fact, there is a large collective of artists, musicians, street performers and theater-makers in the Village. Many artists in the village sell their work on the sidewalk, while musicians strum a tune in local parks and street performers draw crowds in with all the hype they can muster. Decades ago the village was known as a stomping ground for new alternative artists, such as Bob Dylan. And beyond the streets there are plenty of venues within the village to fulfill your desire for culture. Webster Hall, for instance, is one of the most famous concert halls in New York City, hosting bands of new fame alongside the old-schoolers just about every night of the week.

While the Village is a great place to waste the hours of the day, you've got to have somewhere to crash at night. Though there are a few high-rises here and there, most housing options in the village are tenement buildings, usually no more than 6 stories tall. These buildings are historic to the area, as they were some of the first housing built in the early 20th century for immigrant families. Usually, an entire family (or two) would live in one tenement, but they have since been restructured to fit dozens of apartments into one building. Housing prices have been on a steady increase in this area, but if you're not picky about tiny living quarters or multiple roommates, you can usually find something that fits the budget...even if it's just by the skin of your teeth.

So, if you don't mind the hipster crowd and the cost of rent, the village may be the perfect place to lounge in the park, grab some Halal from a street vendor and take in the artistic talents of local street artists to your heart's content.

Midtown West

Danielle Sonnenberg has written for several publications including TheStreet.com, Minyanville.com, and the New York Post. Her blog is blog.daniellesonnenberg.com.

The Good News

1. Accessibility.

The area is near a number of subways. One can get basically get anywhere from midtown west. The subways include: A/C/E/1//Q/N/R. It's called midtown for a reason. It's in the middle of all the action.

1. Affordability.

The further west one goes the cheaper the restaurants are. The area is filled with affordable restaurants from all around the world. Try 123 Shotburger, Eatery, Mee Noodle Shop, Fresco Tortillas and Giorgio's Country Grill.

1. Nature.

Midtown is great for people who want to be in the city but feel like they are at the countryside. The park is a city person's backyard. The Hudson River is also very accessible. In the summer time, one can enjoy kayaking, bike riding and boating.

The Bad News

1. Tourist Central

Expect to see lots of tourists. It's not a residential neighborhood. Attractions such as Museum of Modern Art, Carnegie Hall, Central Park, Radio City Music Hall, and Lincoln Center attract tourists.

1. Not trendy.

Midtown west isn't the trendiest area. Don't expect to see lots of hipsters on a Wednesday evening. It's not an area that one will be excited to brag about to his friends.

1. Gritty.

Some of the area is unsafe. Use caution particularly along 12th avenue and 11th avenue in the 40's and 50's.

Midtown West

When most people think of midtown west, several stereotypes come to mind. Yes, there are lots of tall buildings and finance companies and yes, it does have some of the world's tallest buildings (Conde Nast Building, CitySpire Center, Bank of America Tower) but there's also a strong artistic bent to this side of Manhattan.

The area can be defined from 29th street to 59th street and from Fifth to Eleventh Avenue. Neighborhoods include Hell's Kitchen, The Theater District, Diamond District, Columbus Circle, Garment District and Fashion Center.

The business stereotype is true. Midtown (east and west) is New York's largest central business district after downtown Manhattan. One is likely to encounter the morning rush of commuters at nine in the morning. About 700,000 commuters pile into the midtown area every day bustling to work in their suits, attaches and newspapers.

Just down the block from all these financial companies are several opportunities to view great pieces of art at The Museum of Art and Design, the Museum of Modern Art, and the American Folk Art Museum.

For those who crave dance and theater, the City Center houses several dance companies including Alvin Ailey

American Dance Theater, Paul Taylor Dance Company and also The Manhattan Theater Club.

City Center was opened in 1923 as a meeting hall for the members of the Ancient Order of the Nobles of the Mystic Shrine. The building was going to be demolished but was saved by Mayor Fiorello LaGuardia and City Council President Newbold Morris, who created Manhattan's first performing arts center: a 2,750-seat New York home for the best of theater, music, and dance.

Further West is the Columbus Circle Area. In 2000, the Columbus area completely transformed. The New York Coliseum, which was in the neighborhood for over 40 years was demolished. The Time Warner replaced it. It consists of two 750 ft towers bridged by a multi-story atrium containing upscale retail shops. The Related Companies developed the buildings. The center gives visitors a great opportunity to shop at high-end stores like Hugo Boss, Cole Haan and bebe. Restaurants include: Masa, A Voce, Per Se, Landmarc, and Porter House New York. The shopping center is perfect especially in inclement weather.

The Theater District also known as the Great White Way, is a thin strip of Manhattan, from 53rd to 42nd streets, between Sixth and Eighth Avenue. There are about 36 theaters stuffed into this small area of the city.

Times Square went through lots of changes to get to the state it exists today. From the 1950's to the 1980's it was the center for grindhouse theaters, which showed exploitive films. One of the most famous ones was the Gaiety Theatre, a male strip club that operated for more than 30 years. It wasn't until Giuliani moved in that the area and shut down the theaters in a series of late-night raids by the New York City Police, that the area started to change.

The block of 42nd Street between Seventh and Eighth Avenue has again become home to several legitimate theaters, along with shops and restaurants. This area is now co-signed as "New 42nd St," to make sure people are aware of this change. The area is very safe and welcoming. In the summer time, people can even practice yoga right in the center of Times Square.

About ten blocks down is Pennsylvania Station located on 31st between Seventh and Eighth Avenue. It is one of the busiest rail stations in the world and serves 600,000 passengers a day compared to only 140,000 at Grand Central Terminal, the other rail station, across town.

It was renovated in 1963 to make room for Madison Square Garden, a multi purpose indoor arena. Many were opposed to the destruction as it ruined one of the most important landmarks of the time.

Midtown west is a very convenient and desirable place to live. Those who live in the area can live in several different homes ranging from luxury buildings to townhouses.

A number of subways including the A/C/E/F/B/D/F/N/R/ 9/7 run there. However, it's not a cheap area to live. According to New York Magazine, the average studio sells for $475,000 and rents for $2,500; a one bedroom sells for $812,000 and rents for $3,200.

Universities in the area include New York Institute of Technology, Fordham University at Lincoln Center, John Jay University, and The Keller Graduate School of Management.

Midtown west is a neighborhood that is constantly transforming itself. One of the latest developments in the works is Out NYC Urban Resort, a $30 million 90,000-square-foot complex which will feature several restaurants, bars, a spa, a reception hall, retail stores and dance club, along with a 127-room Axel Hotel.

Essays About Living in New York

I have included a group of essays about living in New York that capture the day to day excitement/sadness/mental growth. The essays are written by two writers who moved to New York. One stayed and one left. Both have interesting things to say.

Amanda Green

Amanda Green is a wonderful writer living in New York. She started blogging her adventures when she moved to New York in 2005 on her blog called the Noisiest Passenger (www.noisiestpassenger.com). She came to New York as part of Teach For America's Harlem program before eventually becoming a full-time writer.

Here I have collected five of my favorite essays she has written about the city. For anyone new to the city or wondering what might await them if they make the plunge Amanda's writing is essential.

Nosiest Passenger

by Amanda Green

The post-work subway ride uptown on Friday is my favorite of the week. I can always get a seat from the Wall Street stop, as people tend to leave their offices earlier. Because we get to sleep late the next day or have fun weekend plans too large for a cubicle, everyone tends to actually look at each other and even smile.

I don't consider my workweek over until I've tutored my last student, Jing, on Friday night. But I do feel lighter. There's a zip of camaraderie among passengers, like we're all in on the same joke or headed to some surprise party someone very high-strung doesn't know about.

A few Fridays ago, I was sitting on the train, listening to music and feeling good. A couple boarded with their toddler, the human equivalent of a sticker burr, a few stops after mine. He clung to his exhausted mom and howled when put down in his own seat.

I locked eyes with the woman sitting across from me. She was coming from a workplace somewhere near mine and had an easy smile barely hidden by Stranger Face, the public "Just get me where I need to be" face. Neither of us needed to say anything to verify a wavelength. If that kid didn't shut up, our Friday evening buzz would be seriously harshed, man.

The mom and dad bent over the toddler to shush him. Strangers shot knowing glances as the boy kept screaming. "Just hold him already!" every passenger silently chided. A 2 train hath more judgment than the pearly gates.

Once on his dad's lap, the squirming child vine fell into a short-lived hush, the calm before the snotty, whining storm. Then he started to scream and thrash like the lead singer of a death metal band.

The woman across from me sent a blinking grimace my way, which I recognized from my days of teaching. In English, it translates to something like, "Do we really need to keep this one alive?"

Does it also take a village to properly beat a child's ass?

The mom looked ready to throw herself from the train. Meanwhile, the dad whipped out a book and started reading aloud.

Saved! The boy stopped crying, I turned down the music pumping from my headphones, and the woman across from me breathed a sigh of relief. Our subway car was collectively proud of this glorious moment in family literacy.

I was just considering letting myself doze a few stops, when the book's plot dissolved or the animal characters became unsympathetic or maybe, maybe the boy was just the spawn of Satan.

Face-clawing, opera-singer-birthing-a-large-breech-pony cries.

Now good friends, give or take never formally meeting, I rolled my eyes at the woman across from me. She rolled hers back. The dad acted quickly and gave the toddler an apple, which he promptly bit into.

"Awww... He was hungry," the fickle audience of passengers realized.

The train surged on in peace. When the boy dropped the apple, everyone braced for the din, but nothing happened. He was curious to see where it rolled and giggled in delight when a girl stopped the fruit's flight with her foot.

The dad took it from her and here's where it became really hard not to talk to strangers. The mom retrieved a tissue and some Purell, gave the apple a cursory wipe, and returned it to the boy. He started eating it. Greedily.

Everyone in the car turned against the parents then. Many people avoid touching the subway pole, which is about 3,000 times cleaner than the floor. Ewww! I've seen vomit, urine, tracked-in animal waste, and garbage on subway floors. I'd never seen anyone eat off of them.

The woman across from me agreed. She wrinkled her nose. When I mirrored the expression, she had to bite the insides of her cheeks to keep from laughing.

Where better to be disgusting than NYC public transportation? For this family, it was no big deal - just another big, dirty apple.

I shook with laughter until I transferred to the local 1 train at 96th Street, where the woman and I sat across from each other again.

In addition to looks, I almost wish we'd exchanged names.

Walk Me to the Subway

by Amanda Green

B. and I dated in March, and our relationship went in like a lamb, out like a lion. Overall, it was gentle. There were lots of movies, plates of seafood, strolls downtown arm-in-arm.

But something was off. And when I found out what it was - after waiting for B. to be ready to tell me what I'd started to figure out - I ended things. He's the sweetest guy. Smart. Adorable. But he was emotionally distant and unable to trust me, and I can't be with a person who can't trust me.

When I told B. I couldn't see him anymore, I was shocked at how upset he was. Tears. Bargaining. Then resignation.

I felt bad that I'd asked him to shave that morning. "It hurts when you kiss me," I said. Without the stubble, B. looked younger. He said he felt naked.

I wanted B. to walk me to the subway from his apartment like he always did, and he asked, "What's the point?"

The point was that sometimes people grow to mean something to you in this way you'd never expect, this way you probably can't even define.

It isn't falling in love. It's deeper than like. Someone just suddenly means something in a city where most everyone is forgettable or like someone else you've known before and liked better.

I wanted B. to walk me to the train station, because it was what we'd been doing for a month. It made that train station mean even more to me than it did after the redheaded boy in the East Village pinned me to a wall and kissed me for the first time. (My heart and my MetroCard fluttered as I caught my train, but not my breath. That was 2006, and special enough I can find the spot on the wall even now).

"Do you really want me to walk you?" B. asked.
"I want you to want to walk me," I said.

He sat and stared at me. We might never see each other again.

With a sigh, B. put on his house slippers. "Come on," he said. We didn't make it all the way across. B. said his heels were touching the street, and that he wanted to turn back early.

"Well, thanks for getting this far," I said. He looked sad. I put my arms around him. "I'm so sorry."

I did what I felt was right for me. But I wished I didn't have to. I wished he would've trusted me. I hoped he'd walk me to the train again sometime. All the way, like he used to.
Because he wanted to.
Last night he did.

It was something.

Familiars on a Train

by Amanda Green

When I broke up with Cade, he left my apartment without hugging goodbye, walked down Central Park West, and disappeared.

For months, I'd look out for him as I walked around the Upper West Side. We didn't live all that far apart - my feet must have covered his tracks myriad times. Then he started working at an office downtown near mine.

But we never saw each other again.

Last Friday, I rushed through the turnstile as the subway pulled into the station. I got on a car farther back from the one I usually ride. The train doors closed. I sat and opened a book.

The train stopped. I kept reading. The train stopped. I looked around. The train started, got to a station, and stopped. The conductor announced that there was a delay due to a sick passenger.

I sat and kept reading until the train was taken out of service. Over the loudspeaker, the announcer yelled to exit. To take the 1 downtown, which wouldn't get me where I needed to be.

I got out with a sigh and saw Cade. Speaking of not getting where you needed to be...

Two years ago, I broke up with him, but that doesn't mean it didn't hurt. Cade was the first serious adult relationship I ever had. He made me want normal things that feel crazy when you're 22 - kids, a house, only one man the rest of my life.

It was new and impulsive and painful. We stayed up too late and together too long. We could never be friends after everything that happened.

Sometimes I thought maybe we'd never really been friends. I told him once I'd just realized we'd never talked about God. Did he believe in a He? Why didn't I know? He shrugged and said, "Sometimes I feel like I just can't talk to you."

Cade and I stood on the platform a few feet apart and said hello. He's now a strange familiar. Like one of those nameless guys you ride the elevator with each day, some neighbor you hear crying through the bedroom wall.

We talked about the sick passenger and the nature of time. He said, "I can't believe this isn't awkward."

"Believe me, any hard feelings I ever had have been passed down to someone else," I replied.

We laughed, and I said, "I'm learning your voice again." I used to hear it in my sleep.

When the 1 train came, we stood next to each other. We creeped downtown and later saw the 2 train back in service across the platform. We quickly dashed to it and sat next to each other.

I told him this would make an excellent short story, but we needed the tension to rise. Something needed to happen. Perhaps a revelation.

Cade shrugged, and I explained it could be someone else's revelation. It didn't have to be one of ours.

We agreed to meet again Sunday.

He bought dinner even when I offered to split it, and then we went to this place a block over for some drinks.

We sat across from each other and Cade said, "I think TBID made a huge mistake when he broke up with you." I know he doesn't like me enough to feel he has to say that, so it meant a lot.

As the night wore on, we talked about the separate failed relationships that followed the one we had.
People didn't love us enough to stay. People said one thing and did another.

When you break up with someone, you sometimes have these fantasies of seeing them again and not giving a damn. This often occurs while listening to Gloria Gaynor.

You see yourself months healed, looking good. Wearing clothes you don't own. Or clothes you own that suddenly fit you better.

Your ex-love looks the same, not better without you. He or she looks at you longingly as you smile, unfettered by grief or regret.

This fantasy will soothe you in three-minute intervals.

But here's what really happens: You'll find each other again randomly. You'll probably be wearing nothing special. You'll be exhausted from staying up too late the night before.

Your ex-love will look how you recall, but will gaze at you with more curiosity than longing.

He'll look pleased to stumble upon the girl who ripped his heart out a few years ago. Then stomped on it. Then blogged about how she stomped on it.

Later, you'll sit across from each other in the dark and laugh. You'll remind him he called you fat. He'll look pained.

He'll get something off his chest he should've said years ago. You would've cared then, but now it's fine. No big deal.

You'll tell him funny ways he haunted you. He'll mention that weird sound you used to make.

No one wants exactly those things back. But something like them with someone else someday would be nice.

Afterward, you'll wait at the subway together for your separate trains. He'll ask if he can pick the lint off your fuzzy black hat. You'll say yes.

You'll look like friends.

His train will arrive. This time he'll hug you goodbye.

The Woman in the Rain

by Amanda Green

It is raining those gentle, but heavy, drops of rain that make me wonder if a macho god is drooling over one too many cleavage-emphasizing sundresses. Because a macho god forever chained to the heavens could get very lonely, no? And looking down all those dresses from so high, dresses worn by women who claim to love Him, could drive Him crazy with longing, no?

At any rate, it begins to rain. From the sandwich shop window, I watch people hurry by. Kids scamper beside parents. A lot of people forgot their umbrellas and don't have to look their best anyway. To hell with it - they pause to window shop. A homeless woman stands against the wall of the store beside the sandwich shop. I've passed it hundreds of times, but couldn't tell you what it sells. Overpriced candles maybe or custom frames. I walk by and never notice. A lot of people walk by and never notice.

The woman is in my line of vision, if I choose to look at her. For awhile I don't. I look at the sidewalk and I wonder where the people who live near me, whom I don't know, are going. I wonder how they afford to live here, how they got here. Shallow as it is, sometimes I wonder what I would choose if I had to take one clothing item each woman is wearing.

A woman is laughing and shrieking with her young daughter. They run hand in hand. They partially cover themselves with large, borrowed raincoats. The little girl's drags the ground. I'm not sure why they don't put the coats on, but they don't. If they did, no one would see the dresses. The mom is svelte in red jersey, the little girl is in something floral. The little girl may never be as beautiful as her mom, and maybe both of them already know this.

They run into the homeless woman, because they aren't looking. The street is theirs; they don't stop before the collision and there are no apologies. Nothing is said. They keep running and cross the street and another and another. And later they are home and dry.

The lady is not, cannot, will not be. I noticed she sounds hoarse with grief or bronchitis. Maybe both. And she's standing, trying to avoid the drops. She asks for help and no one notices her or the store she stands in front of. Thankfully, I see two men stop and give her some money. When I walk out, I give her a dollar. She seems genuinely surprised I've noticed her. I decide her voice is hoarse with grief and bronchitis.

I realize I'm the saddest I've been in a long time.

The Kindness of Strangers

by Amanda Green

There's a low of five degrees today, and a woman gets off the 2 train with no hat, gloves, or scarf. An older man offers her some space under his umbrella, and she graciously accepts.

I walk ahead of them, keeping my eyes down and forward to keep from slipping. Having underestimated the snow, I left my boots at home and am wearing sturdy slip-ons whose color reminds me of dry fall leaves.

The man asks the woman why she isn't more bundled up. She says she wasn't prepared for how cold it would be, much less snow. That makes many of us this morning. We were waiting for night when we'd be out of work, at home or some other place warm and pilled as an old sweater.

"But I'm from Canada," the woman relates. "I'm used to this." The man reckons she is. They stand close together under the umbrella. He towers over her protectively.

The kindness of strangers often has designs. I've had men offer to help me carry heavy boxes from the subway to the street and then ask for some money. Or fawn as they give me directions or make room for me on a bus, concluding the exchange with offers of a date or requests for my phone number. I've purposely misplaced a number of business cards.

In college, I found a guy's wallet once. There's wasn't much in it, but I gleaned plenty of information. His student ID had a small photo, but I couldn't determine whether he was handsome or not. I was attracted, however, to the schedule of classes he'd registered for recently, printed, and folded into a neat square sharper than the one with his picture. Engineering, Japanese, Government. The courses suggested someone with abilities I don't have who likes to challenge himself.

I looked him up in the school directory and sent an email. He replied immediately. I told him he could catch me between classes later at my dorm, which had the convenience of having the school's nicest cafeteria on-site. I mention this not because I considered lunch at Kinsolving to be a classy date, but a meal together could be an option if he was dreamy and whether or not I was hungry.

When we met, I saw how much of a nerd he was and how much of a nerd I am on paper. Maybe he was really inspiring and brilliant, but he just wasn't my type, which was then something like indie-looking boy bander. He seemed kind of interested in me, but I said something like, "You're welcome. I've gotta study now. Bye."

It would've been a sweet way to start something, though.

That's why I slow my pace to eavesdrop and root for the man with the umbrella. The woman talks about the forecast. "Partly cloudy with a 30% chance of a phone number," I think.

She indicates her destination is near, so the man turns in the right place. "Would you like me to walk you to class, too?" he jokes. She laughs and thanks him outside the office building. He wishes her a good day and smiles. His stomach crawls into his throat.

The man takes two quick steps to cross the street and turns back. "Hey, do you wanna have lunch today?" he calls out. I wonder if other people on the sidewalk think they knew each other and are unaware how bold he is.

The woman is holding the door by now; it's heavy in her shivering hands. "No, thanks!" she answers. She walks in the building and doesn't look back.

My heart falls a little, as I imagine his does. But it is nothing compared to the snow around us, a bunch of strangers who every now and then try not to be.

Zachary Wilson

Originally from Brandon, Mississippi, Zachary Wilson had lifelong dreams of New York City. He landed in East Harlem just days after college graduation and quickly began climbing the mountain that is glossy Manhattan magazines. After a few successful years he was abruptly finished and relocated to magical New Orleans. He is now a freelance writer, blogger, and amateur filmmaker. He wrote a wonderful essay about his time in Harlem and what it felt like to be part of gentrification while it is happening.

Above the Upper East Side: I am the Face of Gentrification

by Zachary Wilson

gen·tri·fi·ca·tion (noun) \,jen-trə-fə-'kā-shən\ :: the process of renewal and rebuilding accompanying the influx of middle-class or affluent people into deteriorating areas that often displaces poorer residents.

I am the face of gentrification. It's not something I aspire to be, just something I am. Most of my friends are, too. White kids from middle-class families who have a dream of moving to New York, but the only places they (and their parents) can afford to take root are Harlem, Brooklyn and Queens. But what is it that makes us feel we're safe enough to live in these historically rough areas? Are things really changing? And if so, is New York losing significant pieces of itself in the process?

Standing at the bus stop on East 97th Street and Third Avenue earlier tonight, a black man in his mid-40s was explaining how much things have changed to a woman he was with. "It wasn't always like this," he said, gesturing toward East Harlem, which abruptly starts above 97th Street on the East Side. "Used to, you couldn't catch a yellow cab going this way. You could only catch them if there were coming from up there going down." As he spoke, the light turned green and six yellow taxis drove by, heading uptown. "Getting an apartment up there? Yeah you probably could," he said. "But down there, don't even think about it. Nothing below 97th Street even exists to us."

And it isn't all that untrue. I have two friends who share a studio apartment on East 94th Street and Madison Avenue for $1800 a month. Meanwhile, a mere ten blocks up but seven blocks into Harlem, I pay $1740 for a full two bedroom with a living room and kitchen. We ride the same subway, I just get off one stop after them. How is it possible that the two different areas might as well be two different worlds?

Harlem is a particular place, and you can tell when you enter it. The people change, the buildings change, the stores and restaurants change. Even, in some cases, the street names change: Sixth Avenue becomes Malcom X Boulevard and Lenox Avenue, Seventh Avenue becomes Adam Clayton Powell and Eighth Avenue becomes Fredrick Douglas Boulevard, all named after historical black figures. Is Harlem unsafe? It's debatable either way. Here on the East Side, I feel pretty secure. Walking home from the bus at 2:30 a.m. a few nights ago wasn't the most comfortable I've ever felt, but when an NYPD van drove by and the officer waved at me, I knew my neighborhood was at least being watched. And I see the police patrolling regularly, stopping to disperse groups or check things over.

Whether gentrification is a good thing or a bad thing, I think it's inevitable. Every morning I see young professionals in business attire standing on the subway platform at 103rd Street. And they aren't just white — they're black, white, Hispanic, Asian, Latino, Indian and an infinite number of other races and combinations. And I guess they, or we, are the future of New York, and one day we'll all look back and remember when we lived uptown or across the river. It may not be a high-rise in Midtown or a classic six on the Upper East Side, but it's a start, and an opportunity those who came before me didn't have even a decade ago. All I can hope is that I make it that much better for those who come after me, and that New York's culture will stay in tact in the process.

Made in the USA
San Bernardino, CA
27 September 2013